Setting Boundaries

PUT YOURSELF IN THE DRIVERS SEAT

MARILYN DOWNS

Copyright © 2025 by Marilyn Downs

All rights reserved.

No portion of this book may be reproduced in any form without written permission from the publisher or author, except as permitted by U.S. copyright law.

Contents

Introduction	1
1. Understanding the Need for Boundaries	4
2. Breaking Through Obstacles in Setting Boundaries	17
3. Communication Techniques for Effective Boundaries	30
4. Setting Limits with Various Relationships	42
5. Mindfulness and Self-Reflection Exercises	55
6. Conflict Resolution and Negotiation Strategies	68
7. Creating Customized Action Plans	81
8. Living a Balanced Life by Setting Boundaries	92
References	108

Introduction

I once had one of those moments that changed things forever. I juggled a demanding job, family obligations, and a social calendar that would drive anyone crazy. Driving in my car one night, exhausted and near tears, I thought, "Why am I doing all of this?" It was a moment of clarity from a deep-seated need to please everyone but myself. Then, I realized I had lost control over my life and desperately needed to learn how to set boundaries.

A difficulty far too common in setting personal boundaries is that we are made to believe that we should give all of ourselves to everybody. We say yes when we mean no, and we overcommit out of the sense of disappointing others. We all face setting boundaries, but our society generally supports the belief that success means being busy, therefore allowing little room for personal space.

I had no idea how to set boundaries; my life had been one of those upbringings that created boundary problems. After incorporating boundaries, I found such freedom that this is where my vision for this book comes in. I want to help you with practical tools and ideas for setting boundaries, as this allows you to take charge of your life and have healthier relationships. I aim to empower you toward self-empowerment, where saying no will be as liberating as saying yes. Imagine a life with your needs considered and your time valued. It is easier than you might think.

This book is the place to be if you want to strengthen your relationships; it will point to your needs when you are torn between multiple commitments or running on a treadmill of people-pleasing. We'll delve into the everyday struggles that bind us all.

What's different about this book is its approach, which looks into the mix of psychology and communication skills. You'll find special exercises to understand and set your boundaries. There are scenarios with which you can identify, and you'll have a personalized plan by which you will work for your actual needs. This book isn't a book; instead, it is an on-point - guide for reclaiming your life.

Indeed, this book will bring many added advantages with its reading: knowing oneself better, enhancing people's communication, and even bringing balance to life. Setting boundaries is not just about saying no; it's about making space for what's most important. It's a process that gives rise to serious personal growth.

Think of it more like embarking on a journey of strength and control; it's an invitation to actively engage in the material and apply the strategies in life. Each chapter is another stepping stone, leading you into a future where your needs will be acknowledged and valued.

Here is a quick example of what to expect: First, we will understand why boundaries matter. Then, we'll review real-life communication skills that make setting boundaries easier. We'll look into conflict resolution and mindfulness. Finally, we will conclude with self-reflection lessons to help you stay balanced.

As we begin this journey, remember, you are not alone; I'm here to guide you. Now is the time to take complete control of your life and take it in the direction you want to go.

Chapter One

Understanding the Need for Boundaries

A great poet once said, "Good fences make good neighbors." He probably didn't mean you should start building fences around yourself or putting up velvet ropes at your next family reunion. But seriously, those fences/boundaries are so necessary. Just suppose that in a world in which you go to every gathering, you can meet all those various requests and say yes to every favor in the world with no sweat broken. It's exhausting to contemplate!

Yet, that is how it goes with so many of us. We find ourselves stretched thin, like a rubber band ready to snap, wanting peace. That peace is unreachable without boundaries, and our well-being gets pushed aside.

More than ever, setting boundaries in our world is challenging. We have so many notifications, expectations, and social requirements that we can easily get overwhelmed. We must say yes because we are afraid of judgment or rejection. This endless cycle of people-pleasing leaves us spent.

Visualize the invisible force field called boundaries designed to protect your personal space. They are the traffic lights in relationships, letting you go when it's safe to move forward and stopping you when you need to pause. It's the dos and don'ts you establish with yourself to maintain peace and sanity. They protect your personal space and privacy as physical boundaries; Emotional boundaries help others not trample over your feelings and beliefs as if you were a doormat. Mental boundaries help keep your thoughts and opinions safe and allow you to be yourself without fear.

1.2 Defining Personal Boundaries

Boundaries aren't just about saying no to extra work and declining an invitation to another party. They're about defining what is and isn't acceptable in your life. For example, physical boundaries are not just a matter of personal space in the elevator but also one of your privacy-times alone.

Emotional boundaries, on the other hand, help you protect your feelings and beliefs. They let you show your emotions without fear of being dismissed or invalidated. They ensure that your emotional needs are respected and prioritized.

Mental boundaries protect your thoughts and opinions. They empower you to have your ideas and views, even when they differ from those around you. They allow you to think independently and with confidence, sharing your outlook. Without these mental boundaries, the line between your thoughts and other people's opinions is unclear, and that confusion may lead to self-doubt.

Boundaries are more than emotional and mental realms. Material boundaries protect your stuff and money, ensuring people can't take your things or leech off you financially. They help you say, "No, I don't want to lend you my favorite sweater," or, "I am not in a position to pay for your dinner tonight."

Time boundaries provide balance; they preserve your time and personal space from being commandeered by other people. They allow you to select activities that go hand in hand with your goals and values and leave some time for self-caring and rest. Setting time boundaries could prevent you from burning out, hence leaving space for what matters most in life.

The best thing about boundaries is that they don't need to be inflexible. Indeed, the most flexible boundaries can adapt to life changes as those winds and tides shift. They balance rigidity and flexibility, allowing one to adjust to different situations and relationships. Setting flexible boundaries means realizing that life is temporary; things are ever-changing, and so might one's needs.

Boundaries mean opening up to change and adjusting them if necessary. Acclimatization to changed conditions makes one's boundaries relevant and practical enough to keep harm away from well-being and personal space. By embracing this approach, you help yourself work around relationships and commitments. You take control of your life, creating healthier relationships and earning self-respect. So, as we delve into personal boundaries, remember that these limits are not just fences but keys to a balanced, fulfilling life.

1.3 The Psychology Behind Boundary Issues

When setting boundaries, sometimes our most significant obstacles lie within. Our experiences can create how we perceive and set up those invisible lines. As children, we learn from the environments we grow up in. Family dynamics play a vital role in this learning process. Imagine a household where children are encouraged to express themselves, where "no" is a respected part of the vocabulary. Setting boundaries becomes a natural part of their development in such an environment. However, boundary-setting skills may never develop in a home like mine, where children are supposed to obey and not question authority. As adults, such individuals often feel unable to assert themselves and do not know how to make the line that separates their needs from those of others' demands. Pressure from society is an added layer to the complexity of boundary issues.

Many of us have learned behaviors that value harmony over honesty. We're often taught to avoid disagreements and keep the peace at all costs, sacrificing comfort. That need for approval, instilled within us by society, usually stands as a block to practical boundary setting. The underlying fear is that asserting ourselves risks rejection or conflict. Sometimes, it's just like being caught between a rock and a hard place; you want to keep relationships and avoid disputes, but at what price to your well-being? This internal tug-of-war keeps many from setting boundaries that would actually strengthen their relationships. Not having boundaries is not just an issue in social situations but also in our mental health.

Without clear boundaries, the stress and anxiety can become extreme. Imagine trying to juggle many responsibilities without ever saying no. The result is long-term stress that keeps you up at night and constantly exhausts you. You start to feel emotionally exhausted, and even the most minor tasks begin to feel overwhelming. You may snap on your loved ones or retreat into yourself because you have nothing left to give. With the vicious cycle of no boundaries, emotional overload occurs, making it even more challenging to set those much-needed limits. Psychology can explain why some people struggle more than others.

Attachment theory, for example, makes these dynamics understandable. Secure attachment through which consistent nurturing occurs will generally create an individual comfortable setting boundaries. They know their worth and are confident in expressing their needs. Insecure attachment styles make setting boundaries extremely difficult for the individual. They either cling too tightly to others for fear of abandonment or push people away, unable to trust that their limitations will be respected. These early life attachment styles set the stage for our behaviors by influencing how we interact with the world. This is not about finger-pointing or dwelling on the past when understanding this psychology.

Instead, it is about recognizing the patterns that have shaped us and deciding how to move forward. We can break free from learned limitations by identifying these influences. It's rather like learning a foreign language. It's all so awkward, but eventually, it becomes second nature. We can rewrite the script, substituting the old notions for healthier, empowering ones. Such self-awareness is the first stage of creating something that truly serves us.

1.4 Common Boundary Myths Busted

SETTING BOUNDARIES

Ah, that ancient myth about boundaries being an act of selfishness. Similar to chocolate, but it's not the calorie variety. In reality, the concept of not being greedy with one's boundaries is actually very opposite. It's never about blocking others; it's all about respecting oneself and, then again, everyone else around. Taking care of oneself has gotten bad press ever since it became confused with selfishness. While selfishness would put your needs over everyone else's and potentially harm them, self-care ensures you will be your best self for everyone, including yourself. Imagine an empty pitcher trying to fill glasses—it is not possible. Boundaries help you keep that pitcher full so you have enough to share with others.

The second general myth is that boundaries lead to isolation. In fact, boundaries allow relationships to be stronger and much more real. They are like the invisible threads of a spider's web-delicate yet joined, connecting everything into place. By setting boundaries, you clearly state your needs, reducing misunderstandings and thus building trust. When you are clear about your limits, others feel more comfortable being with you because they know where they stand. This clarity deepens relationships and creates respect, leading to small changes and strength.

Then comes the belief that boundaries are permanent and shall never be altered. This sounds similar to assuming one has to eat only one flavor of ice cream all their lives. Just as taste buds do, boundaries can also evolve. They are not set-in-stone features but guidelines that bend and adjust with your situations and the healthy you of the future. Boundaries change with you. What you need in college may be worlds apart from what you need when working or raising a family. Embracing this ability to change lets you adjust to present needs so that your boundaries remain clear and serve you. Some people think boundaries apply only to a select few.

Boundaries keep everybody, whether introverted, extroverted, or the life of the party centered. It is the structures in a person's life that set up the interactions in daily living so that others do not disrespect your space, time, and energy levels. Again, even extremely outgoing people could find themselves burned out without this. It's like trying to run a marathon on an empty tank; you hit a wall at one point. In the big mix of human connections, boundaries are the threads that ensure the picture holds together in beauty; They are not blockages but pathways leading to understanding and respect.

In debunking these myths, we open ourselves up to the true power of boundaries; they are not instruments of division but tools for connection and self-care. So the next time anyone tells you that boundaries are selfish, smile, knowing that it's actually one of the most generous things you can do for yourself and the people in your life.

1.5 Identifying Boundary Violations

Boundary violations can be as subtle as a whisper or as a neon bright flashing sign. Knowing what they look like is key to maintaining healthy interactions. Try to imagine the scene: you are sitting in a café, having your quiet moment of thought, and somebody not even that acquainted with you pops into your booth. They invade your personal space. This is a classic invasion of boundaries. Not all violations, though, are physical. There's emotional manipulation, where a person uses guilt or flattery to control you when deciding. It's like a puppet on a string, dancing to its tune without consideration for your needs or feelings. The first step in recognition is tuning into one's own emotional barometer.

Often, your gut will tell you that something feels off. You may feel discomfort or resentment when someone crosses the line with you. It's an itch you can't quite scratch, a lingering unease telling you something is incorrect. Guilt is another major red flag. Suppose most conversations wind up with you being coerced into an agreement that has gone against your grain. In that case, those feelings are your psyche, signaling a boundary breach and begging you to act. Letting such violations slide can have profound consequences.

They chafe at your self-esteem over time, and you question your worth and abilities. It's like erosion, wearing away the foundation of your self-confidence little by little. Your stress mounts as you've walked the minefield of other people's expectations, never taking yours into consideration. Perhaps you feel yourself always on edge, waiting for the next transgression. It can be a chronic tension that leads to emotional or even physical exhaustion as you continue to fight, trying to maintain compliance. How do you actually go about effectively dealing with these violations?

It starts with assertive communication, a strong, positively conducted way of communicating your needs clearly and confidently. Imagine a friend who consistently shows up without notice, thus affecting your personal time. You might say something like, "I value our friendship, but I need a heads-up before visits so I can plan my day." This approach respects both your needs and the relationship. Setting clear consequences is yet another approach. In the case of boundary violation, one has to take actions that will reflect or show one's limits: limiting the contact or altering the terms of the relationship, for example.

1.6 Practical Exercise: Boundary Audit

Take a moment to conduct a Boundary Audit. Look at recent interactions and note if there were interactions where your boundary was crossed. Note how this made you feel. Were you uncomfortable, resentful, or guilty? Next, reflect on how you could deal with each of these situations. What assertive communication could you use? What consequences can you set to safeguard against the repetition of boundary violations in the future? This exercise clarifies where your boundaries are and cements the determination to reinforce them. Remember that boundary recognition and response are not merely defensive measures but also proactive toward healthier interactions and self-respect.

1.7 The Role of Boundaries in Empowerment

Like being the ship's captain, charting your course across a great brine. This is what setting boundaries allows you to do: take the tiller of your own ship; boundaries are the rudder that enables you to steer your life in your chosen direction. They allow you to make decisions that align with your values and wants and not at the mercy of others. Setting boundaries means that you are making the rules of the game on what you will or will not accept. Ownership gives you the right to choose, but most importantly, it makes you the master of your voyage and not just a passenger in somebody else's voyage. The more you navigate with boundaries, the more confident and self-assured you become. You start to realize that your decisions, big or small, are yours to make, and that realization is incredibly liberating.

SETTING BOUNDARIES

Boundaries are also closely related to self-respect. When you respect your boundaries, you send a powerful message to yourself and the world that you matter. It is like standing tall and saying, "This is who I am, and these are the lines I draw for my well-being." Such regard for your own well-being fortifies your self-esteem, thus providing a sound bedrock to construct a life. Like any building needs solid grounds to face all tempests, self-esteem needs boundaries to see one through in life. You feel valued and understood when your boundaries are respected, reinforcing your sense of worth. It's a loop of continuous positive feedback: the more you respect your boundaries, the more others do, too, and the more your self-esteem flourishes.

Boundaries protect your present state of being and give way to personal growth. Visualize them as the fertile soil where you can plant your potential seeds. They create a safe space to explore new ideas and take risks without fear of overstepping or being overwhelmed. Clear boundaries let you know where you stand, allowing you to venture into new territories confidently. This safety net encourages you to try new things, learn from your experiences, and grow as an individual. It's like wearing a safety harness while climbing new heights-you can push the limits, knowing your boundaries will catch you if you fall.

Above all, boundaries are protective measures, much like a well-fitted suit of armor. They shield you from emotional and physical harm and put a barrier between you and the slings and arrows of everyday life. Think of them as a force field that keeps negative influences at bay, allowing you to maintain equilibrium and focus on what truly matters. Setting boundaries prevents emotional harm; they protect you from overextending yourself or absorbing others' negativity. They act like a filter, letting in the positive and keeping out the detrimental. This safeguarding preserves your well-being and enhances your resilience, enabling you to face life's challenges with strength and clarity.

1.8 Reflection Exercise: Personal Empowerment Blueprint

Take a few minutes to develop your Personal Empowerment Blueprint. List areas where you feel empowered, identifying the boundaries supporting this empowerment. Then, identify areas where you may feel less in control and list boundaries that you could reinforce or establish. Reflect on how these changes might affect your self-esteem and personal growth. This exercise will help shed light on the power of boundaries in your life and how to take ownership of your choices. Remember, boundaries are not just lines in the sand; they are the pillars you lean on to construct a life of empowerment and self-respect.

1.9 Understanding Your Unique Boundary Needs

Understanding your unique boundary needs begins with introspection, like having a heart-to-heart with yourself. It's about acknowledging what your space really needs to keep you healthy. One great tool for reflection like this is journaling. Visualize yourself sitting down with a cup of tea, pen in hand, as you wander through your mind. Ask yourself, "When do I feel most drained?" or "What situations make me uncomfortable?" Just write freely and let your thoughts cascade without judgment. This exercise can show patterns in your interactions, underlining where your boundaries need strengthening. By being more aware of your experiences, you can identify areas where you need stronger boundaries. This practice makes clear what your needs are and how to act in the direction of aligning your life with those needs. Journaling is a mirror to your innermost desires and helps you chart a course toward healthier relationships.

Personal values form the backbone of your boundary needs. They act like a compass guiding your decisions and interactions. Like a well-tuned orchestra, life feels more harmonious when boundaries align with your core values. For instance, you might set boundaries around truthful relationship communication if you value honesty. Conversely, if family is paramount, you may prioritize time boundaries to ensure quality moments with loved ones. The alignment of boundaries with values ensures that your actions are congruent with who you are and thus fosters authenticity and integrity. This then acts as a filter that helps you decide what you accept and reject. In this way, decision-making can become intuitive when your boundaries reflect your values, hence decreasing stress and increasing satisfaction. You find yourself saying yes to things that matter and no to those that don't, creating a life that resonates with your deepest beliefs.

Creating a personalized boundary framework is like designing your blueprint for how you engage with the world. This involves crafting strategies that cater specifically to your lifestyle and personality. You tailor-make your boundary approach to fit your unique contours, like a tailor-fitted suit. An introvert would factor this into setting aside quiet time to get recharged. At the same time, for an extrovert, it would be a question of not burdening people with too much of themselves, yet ensuring they get what they need from their socialization. Setting personal boundaries means being considerate that one size does not fit all, meaning embracing one's uniqueness and setting boundaries that nurture. The tailored method through which you get to lead your life with incredible confidence and clarity in the knowledge that your boundaries serve the very purpose for which they were set, being able to reach out to the world on your terms and make relationships where people respect and honor the unique you. There are different needs for boundaries, just like the people setting them.

Different personalities and lifestyles demand distinct boundaries, like how different plants require unique conditions to flourish. For example, someone with a demanding job may need strict boundaries to protect their time. At the same time, students might focus on boundaries supporting their academic pursuits. An artist needing creative freedom might set boundaries that limit distractions, allowing inspiration to flow uninterrupted. Appreciating these differences shows the very personal nature of setting boundaries. One-size-fits-all won't happen; people's boundaries come from their lives and individual choices. With such information, one makes empathetic and respectful relations, in which appreciation is extended toward the uniqueness of others' needs. This allows for effective communication and cooperation, ensuring one feels heard and valued. As you explore your boundary needs, remember that this is a process not of building walls but of building bridges to a more fulfilling life.

It's about creating spaces where you can flourish, supported by boundaries that honor your true self. Embrace this opportunity to reflect, align, and personalize your boundaries, knowing that in doing so, you are crafting a life that celebrates your individuality and nurtures your well-being. Your boundaries are not lines but a basis on which one builds a life of balance, respect, and empowerment.

Chapter Two

Breaking Through Obstacles in Setting Boundaries

Scenario: You sit down to dinner with your family, and someone brings up politics. You instantly feel your stomach knot because you know where this will go. You instinctively smile, nod, and try to change the topic. The fear of conflict is one of the more common obstacles in setting boundaries. Many of us grew up in environments where conflict was swept under the rug or exploded like fireworks on the Fourth of July. You may have had a front-row seat to arguments that made you want to crawl under the table. Such experiences often teach us to avoid conflict like the plague. But here's the kicker: avoiding conflict doesn't make it disappear; it just pushes it deeper inside, where it festers like an unresolved math problem.

Our upbringing dramatically influences how we perceive and deal with conflict. Some of us may have grown up around hostile environments, meaning loud and aggressive disagreements. This sets up a blueprint to view conflict as bad and uncomfortable. We learn avoidance behaviors as a result: subtle, crafty ways to avoid confrontations. Almost like a ninja, dodging an oncoming disagreeable situation with perfect finesse, never being met head-on in an argumentative position. Tactics that may serve to avoid an actual, external conflict often work to create an internal tumult. Suppressing emotions to prevent conflict may make one anxious and undermine self-esteem, per Psychology Today. It's like trying to hold a beach ball underwater: the pressure builds until it inevitably resurfaces, sometimes with more vigor than before.

However, conflict is not the villain it is made out to be. It's a necessary ingredient in healthy relationships. Constructive conflict is the soil upon which growth takes root. It allows individuals to express differing opinions, expanding perspectives and fostering understanding. It has all the earmarks of a challenging relationship workout: exhausting yet oddly strengthening. In contrast, Destructive conflict is the tornado variety-mesmerizing until it tears the roof off emotional security and everything else in the family. The primary key to any of this is how this conflict worked with and/or transformed from destructive to constructive conversation.

With each conflict, use tools that promote open, respectful communication. In this respect, active listening is a potent exercise: it means listening not merely to respond but to understand the other person's point of view. You are an archaeologist digging out the meaning buried beneath the words. Focusing on the other person's perspective creates an atmosphere where both individuals feel heard and appreciated. Another tool is using "I" statements to express your feelings.

Instead, say, "You always ignore my texts," say, "I feel overlooked when my messages go unanswered." This shifts blame to personal experience and defensiveness and opens up a door to honest dialogue.

Some real payoffs come with confronting conflict head-on. It's like cleaning out a closet: daunting at first but deeply satisfying. Addressing conflict strengthens relationships by building stronger communication skills and enhancing mutual understanding. It is like wiping a foggy window; you can see clearly and appreciate the view once the mist disappears. Successfully navigating conflict may enhance self-confidence, reinforcing the sense of standing firm in your boundaries and asserting your needs. It reminds us that conflict is not an enemy but a stepping stone toward more genuine and satisfying contact.

2.2 Reflection Exercise: Conflict Assessment

Now, take some time and think of a recent conflict that did not sit well with you. Document what initiated the conflict, how you acted, and whether there were behaviors related to avoidance. Consider what else might have been done using active listening or "I" statements. It enables one to observe patterns and try new ways of handling conflict. Conflict does not need to be anxiety-provoking but an opportunity to learn and grow. Relationships, like a garden, blossom even through challenges when tended to.

2.3 Guilt and Selfishness

Ah, guilt-so many of us have been socially programmed to feel this way in setting boundaries through societal and family expectations that raise self-sacrifice onto a pedestal of virtue. Most cultures elevate putting others first as the height of kindness. But that gets you into a pattern where you constantly put others first while your needs gather dust. This pressure to live up to such expectations may raise an internal battle wherein setting boundaries feels like a betrayal of the values one has been so indoctrinated with. It's as if you were in a tug-of-war, but the rope was made from guilt and self-doubt.

A differentiation that stands out for overcoming guilt is between self-care and selfishness. Self-care is not about indulging in endless spa days or taking vacations that make your Instagram followers green with envy. It's about recognizing and honoring your needs and ensuring you have what you need to be your best emotionally and physically. Setting boundaries is an act of self-respect and self-care. Think of it as putting on your oxygen mask first to help others. It's not just an airplane rule; it's a life rule. By setting boundaries, you are not closing people out but creating space to grow, making you more present and available for meaningful interactions. Selfishness means your needs first, no matter what others need or how it will affect them. It's like eating the last piece of cake without asking if anyone else wants any. Boundaries are not about excluding people; they are about including yourself in the big picture of life.

Guilt management is all about rephrasing and reorganizing thoughts and perceptions. Cognitive restructuring means identifying and challenging those beliefs that make you feel guilty about setting boundaries. First, start to question your inner narrative of yourself. Ask yourself, "Why am I feeling guilty saying no, and whose expectation am I trying to meet?" As you unpack these thoughts, you can start unwinding the web of guilt and replacing it with a different thought pattern. Positive affirmations also fall in: remind yourself that it is okay to put yourself first and say, "I deserve to have my needs met" or "The setting of boundaries is an act of kindness both to myself and others. This is like changing old, worn-out shoes with ones that fit, which comfort and support as one walks through life.".

2.4 A mindset shift in encouraging:

Boundaries are not barriers but bridges toward better relationships. By setting boundaries, you are being kind to yourself and acknowledging your worth and valid needs. This helps dissolve guilt and makes setting boundaries an empowering rather than weakening experience. Think of a gardener whose boundaries are the fence that protects his garden and allows it to thrive. If he had a wall, his plants would be tended to, as would his needs. Reframe boundaries for yourself as an act of love that will protect you and give much more to whom you want to, with less resentment and fatigue. You'll show up in your complete authenticity for those who mean so much to you.

2.5 Tactics for People Pleasers

Visualize a scene of yourself standing in a crowded room, nodding to every request. Your head bobs like a buoy in a sea of obligations trying to stay afloat. That scene is very much like a people-pleaser. Saying no is simply a problem and usually characterizes people-pleasers.

It's as if "yes" has been tattooed on their foreheads. They typically have this compulsive urge to agree for fear of simple refusal shattering their relationships. This tendency extends to overextending themselves; obligations pile up, leading to a calendar as packed as a holiday fruitcake.

The drawbacks of people-pleasing are as plentiful as the requests you keep agreeing to. Emotional exhaustion sets in like a constant fog that refuses to lift. You're drained from juggling commitments that aren't even yours to hold. You become overcommitted, and you're just wondering when your needs will ever be addressed for once. This creates a cycle that can easily result in burnout, leaving you without energy or enthusiasm. Relationships suffer because resentment and frustration affect how you relate to others.

But never fear; change is achievable. Just imagine yourself taking small steps toward insisting on your needs without feeling guilty. This gets you to practice saying no in a very safe environment, and it's much like rehearsing for a play, trying new lines and gestures. Gradual exposure can be amazingly transformative in saying no. Start with low-stakes situations, such as when an invitation to coffee feels too much, and you'd rather have an evening at home. Each time you assert your needs, you build stronger muscle with use. With time, this practice makes you more comfortable and confident in setting your boundaries.

The long-term benefits accompanying decreasing people-pleasing tendencies are a breath of fresh air. You will be afforded increased personal time, a pretty valuable commodity today. Imagine having the liberty to choose how to spend your day without being tied down to demands from people around you. Less overcommitting brings in more energy and excitement about essential things. Relationships improve; authenticity replaces resentment. Generally speaking, people will actually appreciate your honesty, and you'll attract people who respect your boundaries. You're an architect of your life, designed to have your values and priorities honored.

2.6 Interactive Element: The No-meter

Now, create a "No-meter." Draw a simple gauge on paper or in your journal. Label one end "Always Say Yes" and the other "Comfortable Saying No." Reflect on recent conversations you have had, and place yourself on that gauge. What is your tendency? Challenge yourself: Try to be one step closer to "Comfortable Saying No" this week. Observe your process and note any thoughts or difficulties. This is a light-hearted yet potent activity to visualize growth and acknowledge each step toward balancing the scale of life.

2.7 Anxiety and Boundary Setting

Close your eyes and picture yourself standing on the side of a diving board above the pool. You're unsure if the water is icy or warm, which can freeze you in place. Setting boundaries feels similar. Anxiety surrounds it, real anxiety, most of the time associated with a fear of adverse outcomes. You may fear others' reactions or rejection. It's like handing over your favorite book to someone who may or may not appreciate it as much as you do. This fear of the unknown can be paralyzing, keeping you from asserting yourself and establishing the boundaries you need.

But taking heart is a tool to help manage this anxiety. Breathing exercises are a simple yet powerful way to calm the nerves. Picture this: you close your eyes, take a deep breath, and slowly exhale. It's like hitting the reset button on your panic. Breathing deep can help calm the mind and body, making it easier to approach boundary-setting with a clear head. Visualization techniques are also practical. Imagine a scenario where you set a boundary with confidence. Visualize the conversation going smoothly, with both parties understanding and respecting each other. The practice can make you more prepared and less anxious when setting those boundaries.

Incremental progress is essential when it involves managing anxiety. Think of building a sandcastle one bucket at a time: you do not have to create a fortress all at once. You may want to take small steps or micro-boundaries. These are small limits you can set that feel manageable. It could be as simple as telling a friend you can't hang out because you need some alone time. Your confidence grows like a plant reaching for the sun as you practice setting these micro-boundaries. Every successful boundary increases your self-assurance, making it easier to tackle more significant challenges.

Sometimes, hearing how others have successfully managed anxiety and set effective boundaries can be incredibly motivating. Consider the young woman who felt inundated with work. She constantly agreed to extra shifts out of fear that saying no might jeopardize her position. She slowly reached a breaking point, knowing something had to give. Then, she set a boundary with her lunch break, ensuring she took it uninterrupted. The positive result gave her confidence to establish boundaries, such as refusing extra shifts that didn't suit her schedule. Her anxiety decreased, and she was able to find a balance between taking care of her work commitments and her personal well-being. With those first few actions, she actually transformed her anxiety into empowerment, learning that setting boundaries didn't have negative consequences but, in fact, made her life much better.

2.8 Visualization Exercise: Calm Confidence

Find a quiet place and sit comfortably. Close your eyes and take a deep breath. Imagine yourself in a situation where setting a boundary may arise. Visualize speaking calmly, clearly, and sincerely in your words. Imagine the other person listening well and saying yes to your needs. Let the anxiety go as the conversation goes well. Hold this image, using it to reinforce confidence. Open your eyes now, knowing this calm confidence can be taken into real-life interactions. Return to this exercise whenever anxiety creeps in to further solidify the resolve for boundary setting.

2.9 Dealing with the Fear of Loss of Relationships

Imagining that one is on a tightrope, juggling between pleasing others and not compromising one's well-being, the fear of losing relationships could be the gust of wind that may knock them off the rope. It's a common worry—setting boundaries might mean losing the people you care about. However, this fear is based on misconceptions. The idea that boundaries lead to rejection is a myth. Understanding that boundaries can enhance relationships is key to overcoming this fear.

Studies indicate that healthy boundaries often strengthen relationships rather than weaken them. This would be an environment of trust and equality when both parties understand and respect each other's limits. Research shows that participants who established clear boundaries reported higher relationship satisfaction than those who did not. These findings suggest that boundaries act to frame mutual respect. They provide clarity that prevents misunderstandings and resentment from building up. In setting boundaries, you are not pushing people away but inviting them into a space where both of you can thrive. It's just like in a well-tended garden; every plant will get its room to grow and flourish.

Communication will help you ease these fears of losing relationships. You use empathetic ways of communication to express your needs without alienating others. This can be framed by saying, "I value our friendship, and I want to make sure we both feel comfortable." This approach helps the other individual to be more confident that your motive is not to retreat but to have better quality in your relationship. It is like adjusting a radio volume—the conversation should be clear and pleasant but not blaring or silent. By approaching these conversations with empathy, you will create a space where boundaries connect points, not lines.

Take some time for self-reflection to help identify which relationships truly serve your growth. You may want to do a relationship inventory in which you look at the dynamics of your interactions. Ask yourself, "Does this relationship lift and support me?" and "Do I feel valued and respected?" It helps by understanding the level at which each relationship nurtures personal growth in your life, including which ones are worthy of revisiting. In that way, it is akin to cleaning your closet and separating what is or isn't serving you. This process helps you become focused on your energy and invest it in relationships that nourish your life while setting boundaries to support and protect those relationships.

This means it takes a different mindset in which the fear of losing relationships must be changed. Boundaries are not barriers but bridges to more profound connections. They give you the structure to maintain healthy and fulfilling relationships where both parties feel respected and valued. This kind of thinking, coupled with sympathetic communication, will allow one to break through the barrier of fear and build connections that support growth and well-being.

2.10 Breaking Loose from Social Conformity Pressures

Now, imagine yourself in the stage of life where everybody seems to be reading from the same script, smiling politely, nodding at every suggestion, and moving with the crowd. Social conformity is that invisible director that guides our actions with promises of acceptance and belonging. And on your shoulder is this powerfully whispered voice that says, fit in with others; get acceptance, likes, and everything good. And to feel accepted this firmly may push out of our needs and often wants, pushing ourselves to accommodate to keep up the harmony in life. At that moment, it is certain to overlook and be lost under all the pressure and noise coming from others about us.

Please think of the high school students who joined a popular club not because they were interested in it but because everyone else was doing it. They would sit at the meetings and listen to discussions for hours without personal interest. Or think of the employee who agrees to an office tradition of after-work drinks, even when they'd prefer to head home to decompress. These scenarios show the strong yet subtle pressure toward conformity, where saying no is like swimming against a current that pulls you back into the status quo. The result of such a life is one that others' expectations, not personal values or preferences, have dictated. It's like wearing shoes that don't quite fit and are uncomfortable, yet you keep them on because everyone else is wearing the same pair.

It does take a combination of assertiveness and self-awareness to overcome such pressures toward conformity. The practice of being assertive is finding the courage to say, "This is what I need," and standing firm on that declaration. It's to know your voice counts, even when it opposes the majority. You can enhance this resolution by building a supportive community around you, people who respect and encourage your individuality. Think of them like your cheering squad, ready to back you up when the crowd roaring gets too loud. These allies remind you that being true to yourself is worth more than any fleeting approval.

Developing a personal value system acts as your North Star through the fog of societal expectations. Developing a personal mission statement might seem like a potent exercise in this process. First, decide upon what really means something to you in your life. What things do you want to stand by, no matter the influence from around you? Write them somewhere where you can easily have them in view, like in your mirror or cell phone. A mission statement always keeps one in mind about his core values, making decision-making clear and sure. It's like having a map that keeps you on course, even when the path gets rocky.

In breaking loose from social conformity, you unlock the gates to a life that's genuinely yours. You engage in the world not as a shadow of what others would expect but as a vibrant expression of your uniqueness. It is that feeling of liberation, like taking off heavy clothes on a hot day and confidently moving freely. As you enter this new empowerment, your relationships deepen, your sense of self strengthens, and the world becomes a richer tapestry of possibilities.

Chapter Three

Communication Techniques for Effective Boundaries

Imagine yourself as a juggler, juggling flaming torches of commitments, expectations, and the occasional unsolicited advice. Every day, you dance around things so that everything stays up in the air without you getting burned. And yet, amidst the chaos, one skill can turn this juggling act into a symphony of harmony: saying no. It's a two-letter word with exceptional potency and is often as elusive as a unicorn. Saying no is an important communicative tool, especially when setting boundaries. It is not about saying no to others; it's yes to yourself and what is important or a priority to you.

A clear and direct "no" should not be underestimated. It's like a beacon, guiding the ships around the rocks of overcommitting. A

SETTING BOUNDARIES

no, socially, could spare you a whole weekend of regretful yeses, like having to attend the birthday party of your neighbor's cat. At the same time, you stay curled up with your favorite novel. Saying no with assertiveness in professional life is essential to sustaining your sanity and productivity. Refraining from accepting additionna work you cannot do means that you produce quality work without diluting your efforts in too many different areas of commitment.

But let's face it, saying no can be awkward and sometimes downright uncomfortable. It's like trying to fit into jeans two sizes too small, but not without a struggle. There are ways to soften the impact. Phrases like "I can't commit to that right now" or "I'm not available currently, but thank you for thinking of me" convey the same message without the bluntness. These options keep you in politeness while you firmly draw boundaries; you can say no and not feel like you are the villain in a melodrama. You are not slamming the door but simply allowing the right guests in.

Much of the discomfort with saying no comes from fear of disappointing others. It's a universal anxiety on par with concerns about being picked last for kickball. The key is to practice with low-stakes scenarios, such as declining a second helping of Aunt Mildred's mystery casserole. You start building confidence, learning the world does not end when you say no. Over time, you graduate to more significant challenges: saying no to a request to chair yet another committee at work or school.

Repetition is your friend in perfecting this skill. Like riding a bike, the more you practice, the easier it gets. Role-playing exercises with friends are peculiarly helpful; they provide an opportunity to safely try out one's no and smooth down delivery while receiving valuable feedback. Visualize your friend being a stand-in for that boss or that nagging classmate - a way of rehearsing your responses and getting them right on target in real time. These exercises desensitize the fear of rejection by turning that dreaded no into a usable and empowering tool.

3.2 Interactive Element: No Practice Chart

Develop a "No Practice Chart" to track your progress. Draw a simple table with columns for "Request," "Response," and "Outcome." Each time you say no, jot down the details. Reflect on how it felt and note any changes in your comfort level over time. Refer to this chart as a visual reminder of your growth and a motivator to continue refining your skills. You will see how each no tells a story of empowerment and self-respect, taking the most straightforward word in English and rendering it into a potent assertion of the boundary.

3.3 Language Tools for Clear Communication

Just think about being at a family gathering and having Aunt Edna, like a detective with a magnifying glass, not stop pressing you with personal questions. Squirming out is a natural temptation, but the assertive use of language comes to the rescue at this point. The assertive use of language is one's Swiss Army knife-very versatile and able to handle any challenging boundary. The cornerstone of assertive communication rests on "I" statements. These gems allow you to express personal needs without pointing fingers or starting a feud. Instead of saying, "You always ask too many questions," try, "I feel overwhelmed when asked too many personal questions." This approach focuses on your feelings, reducing defensiveness and encouraging understanding.

Think of all the times when you have to draw the line, be it telling a roommate you need quiet time or telling a colleague you're uncomfortable with specific tasks. This is where effective boundary language comes in handy. Phrases like "I need some time to myself" or "I'm not comfortable with that" are straightforward yet respectful. They honor your needs while maintaining the dignity of the person you're speaking to. These statements are soft yet clear boundaries that others can perceive without feeling insulted. Using precise language creates a mutual understanding that respects everyone's space and needs.

The tone and intonation of your voice can make a simple statement sound like poetry or a declaration of war. Compare asking for a day off in a timid whisper versus a confident tone. The message remains the same, but the reception changes dramatically. In boundary communication, it is essential to practice calm and firm tones. It is like the difference between a gentle stream and a roaring river: both carry water, but one is so much more soothing. The calm tone invites cooperation, while the firm tone underlines seriousness without aggression. This balance will ensure your message gets through clearly and respectfully, creating an atmosphere of mutual understanding.

Consistency in language is the unsung hero of effective boundary-setting. Think of a chameleon-always changing color. Sure, it's interesting, but it's also unpredictable. In communication, inconsistency can lead to confusion and mixed messages. If you communicate a boundary one day and then contradict it the next, others may have a hard time taking your boundaries seriously. Consistent language reinforces your boundaries over time. Setting a metronome to the tempo of your message keeps it on an even keel; it keeps the message clear and steadfast. By not sending mixed messages, you build trust in your communication, making it easier for people to respect your boundaries.

3.4 Textual Element: Case Study

Consider Lucy, who had problems with setting boundaries at work. She would often say yes to tasks beyond her capacity and burn out. By instilling assertive language, she learned to communicate her limits clearly. She non-judgmentally utilized "I" statements: "I feel overwhelmed with my current tasks, and I need to focus on my priorities." Due to the course of time, her clarity of communication and even tone of voice received respect and consideration from her coworkers since she could handle her responsibilities without compromising her well-being. Lucy's situation is an apt example of how assertive language can create change by setting boundaries.

3.5 Non-Verbal Cues and Boundaries

Now, put yourself in a situation where you must describe an entire story without saying a word. That is the power of non-verbal communication, and setting boundaries may spell volume. How you hold your body, where your eyes land, and even how you stand can all scream as loudly as words. Let's begin with eye contact. It's like the Wi-Fi connection between two people; when strong, it conveys confidence and sincerity. Direct eye contact tells others that you mean business, you are firm in your boundaries, and you are not to be trifled with. It's a silent assurance that you are present and into it, making it hard for anyone to dismiss your words.

The other significant player in this orchestra of non-verbal communication is posture. Now, picture someone standing tall with their shoulders back and spine straight. This is confidence and assertion, meaning you control your space. Now, contrast it with a hunched-over figure with eyes lower than the toes, as if they are apologetic for taking up space. The stance can then be undermined where your boundaries don't look binding.

On the other hand, standing tall reinforces your verbal messages. It serves as a visual key that you are firm and grounded. It is like the exclamation point at the end of a sentence, unmistakable and definitive.

Non-verbal signals go beyond posture and eye contact. Consider crossed arms, a universal symbol of discomfort or defensiveness. This gesture can reinforce the message that certain behaviors are not welcome when setting boundaries. It is a physical barrier, a silent "no entry" sign. But be aware that context counts. Crossed arms can also denote coldness or a comfortable stance. These signals need attention to the broader context and the individual's normal behavior. One may get more from observing facial expressions. A furrowed brow or pursed lips could mean they don't understand or are in disagreement, helping you to modulate your communication about how your limits are being taken in.

Learning to read the non-verbal signs of others is a superpower that allows you to bring real-time modulation into your communication. Suppose you explain a boundary and notice the other person avoiding eye contact or fidgeting. These cues may indicate discomfort or disagreement. By picking up on these signals, you can pause, clarify your intentions, or ask for feedback to ensure you've conveyed your message. The ability to read non-verbal cues helps you communicate better and address concerns that aren't spoken while setting boundaries. The effectiveness of setting boundaries depends on how well verbal and non-verbal communication align. Think of it as a dance: the message is clear and cogent when both are in sync. When you say, "I'm comfortable with this arrangement." Still, your body language screams otherwise; the disconnect can plant doubt and confusion. When your gestures, posture, and facial expressions match your words, you have a cohesive message that others can understand. Consistent messaging through gestures underlines the gravity of your boundaries, making them less likely to be challenged. It's the difference between a symphony and a cacophony-one resonates while the other disrupts.

3.6 Dealing Gracefully with Negative Reactions

Setting boundaries can sometimes feel like navigating a minefield, especially when the potential for adverse reactions looms. Preparing for these situations is essential, much like a meteorologist anticipating a storm. Your first line of defense is to recognize defensive behaviors. Visualize someone crossing their arms, raising their voice, or responding curtly. Most of the time, these are signs of defensiveness, a natural reaction when one feels that his space or autonomy is being challenged. Instead of taking it personally, use this as a chance to reinforce your boundaries with clarity and calmness. Anticipation is not about expecting the worst but being prepared to understand and respond appropriately.

De-escalation techniques are essential during heated situations that challenge your limits. Think of soothing language as a balm for heated exchanges. Phrases like "I understand this is different for us" or "Let's talk about this calmly" can defuse tension and invite a more rational conversation. In addition, it is essential to keep calm. You are the eye of the storm—the quiet center of turbulence. Your composure can have a soothing effect on others, signaling that you're open to dialogue and resolution rather than conflict. Deep breathing helps sustain this calm; it signals your brain to relax, allowing you to respond thoughtfully rather than impulsively.

Empathy is another cornerstone of effective boundary communication. Putting oneself in another person's shoes enables one to understand another person's perspective. Perhaps they feel rejected or are confused by your new assertiveness. Validation of feelings, even when one disagrees with them, respects a person's experience. You could say, "I can see this is a surprise, and I appreciate your willingness to talk about it." This reiterates your boundary yet acknowledges their feelings, creating a space for respect and understanding.

Besides empathy, self-regulation is essential in managing your emotional response to a negative reply. When someone resists your boundary, it is easy to become defensive or hurt. Deep breathing exercises can be a lifeline here, anchoring you into the present and keeping your emotions in check. It's as if with every inhalation, serenity comes into your body, and tension leaves your body with each exhalation, each step closer to achieving balance of mind. This helps you get through such moments and slowly trains you to resist adversities and tackle frustrating interactions elegantly. We are imperfect, and we make plenty of mistakes:

Take a moment and reflect on a recent situation where your boundaries were challenged. What defensive behaviors did you notice, and how did you respond? Were there opportunities to use de-escalation techniques or express empathy? Jot down your thoughts and consider how you might approach similar situations. This exercise encourages self-awareness and helps identify areas for growth, transforming negative encounters into learning experiences.

3.7 Assertiveness Without Aggression

The concepts of assertiveness and aggression get intertwined into the same basket and can't be separated further. Imagine that assertiveness is like a firm but soft handshake, a manner of communicating in which one expresses one's needs without stepping on people's toes; it's expressing oneself honestly but respecting others simultaneously. Aggression, however, is like a bull in a china shop. It's aggressive and forceful and often leaves a trail of broken relationships. Where assertiveness builds bridges, it burns them down. Understanding this distinction is key to maintaining healthy interpersonal dynamics.

Let's look at some examples of assertive communication. Say your friend keeps 'borrowing' your favorite books, never returning them. You're running a library that has a no-return policy. Instead, an assertive response would be, "I like sharing my books, but I would appreciate it if you could return them after you are through with them so that others can have a chance to read them too." This response is firm yet polite. It clearly states the boundary without accusing your friend of being a book thief. Similarly, suppose a colleague constantly interrupts you in meetings at work. You might say, "I appreciate your ideas, but I'd like to make my point before we move forward." This states your need for respect and opens up an avenue for cooperation.

The advantages of assertiveness are not limited to setting boundaries. It actually strengthens relationships by cultivating an atmosphere of respect. When you communicate assertively, you are, in essence, letting the other person know that you respect both your needs and theirs. This balance strengthens the foundation of any relationship, whether personal or professional. Assertiveness also boosts self-respect. Standing up for oneself reinforces one's worth and sets a good precedent for others regarding treatment. This is like sowing seeds of confidence, which grow into a garden of self-assurance.

Assertiveness is developed through a process involving self-discovery and practice. The use of self-affirming exercises can be one of the strong tools in this process. Write positive statements about yourself, such as "I have the right to express my needs" or "My feelings are valid and important." Repeat these affirmations daily, letting them sink into your subconscious. Over time, they'll become a natural part of your thought process, bolstering your confidence in asserting your boundaries.

Another approach would be to practice assertive language in daily interactions: start with small scenarios, like ordering a coffee or making a request at the store. Be direct and clear in the language, and notice how it feels. Gradually, apply those skills to more challenging situations, like discussing workload with a boss or addressing personal boundaries with family. Each interaction is an opportunity to refine your approach, making assertiveness a more natural and comfortable part of your communication style.

As with riding a unicycle, becoming assertive takes time and patience. You may wobble, but then you'll balance. Remember that being assertive doesn't mean you get your way at all costs; it means standing firm in your values while respectfully considering the rights of others. You will develop empowerment with this skill, enriching your relationships and enhancing your self-worth.

3.8 Reinforcing Boundaries Over Time

Setting boundaries acts like planting a garden. While planting gets it all started, maintaining and nurturing the garden enables it to flourish. Reinforcement is thus essential in keeping boundaries intact and effective. If left unattended for a long time, erosion of boundaries will set in, just like a garden that, if uncared for, takes over with weeds. This erosion can be subtle; others may gradually test the limits or forget the boundaries you set. Therefore, setting them is not a one-time declaration but an ongoing commitment to yourself. It means reminding yourself and others that these boundaries count and are here to stay.

One of the ways you can keep your boundaries strong is by frequent self-checking. These can be thought of as maintenance sessions for your emotional well-being. Take a few moments each week to review how your boundaries are holding up. Where are they being disregarded or pushed? In what ways are you being overextended, and where are you maintaining your balance? These reflections enable you to make adjustments where necessary so that your boundaries can continue to work for you. Equally important is the reiteration of your boundaries when necessary. It's like putting on sunscreen on a sunny day once is not enough. Gently remind them when others don't remember your limits and why the boundaries are there.

It's as sure as rain on a parade that challenges to keep boundaries intact will occur. Constant reinforcement makes the process of reinforcement feel Herculean at best. There are people who quite willingly or willfully push their luck with boundaries to determine how far those boundaries can go. Challenges, if they come forth, indeed merit firmness along with consistency. It may be direct conversations where you remind them of your boundaries or an action where the boundaries are continually breached. Remember, having boundaries does not make you difficult; it means you love and respect yourself. It's setting a line in the sand and sticking to it, even when the tide of persistence tries to wash it away.

Reminders and self-reflection are strong allies in this process. Writing down boundary experiences can be pretty enlightening. Consider keeping a boundary journal where you write down the times when your boundaries were challenged or maintained. Reflect on those experiences, observing patterns and areas for growth. Not only does this practice fortify boundaries, but it also helps the individual develop self-awareness regarding how to deal with such situations in the future. This is a personal chronicle of growth, as boundaries have continuously changed and strengthened over time.

As we close this chapter, remember that reinforcement over time is about protecting your space and nurturing your well-being. Consistent reinforcement allows your garden of boundaries to thrive, creating space for growth and development. Moving on, let's see how to apply these principles in different life contexts and make boundaries a natural part of your daily interactions for the betterment of personal and professional relationships.

Chapter Four

Setting Limits with Various Relationships

Picture the scene: You are at a family reunion, and suddenly, Aunt Mildred starts quizzing you about every life decision you have ever taken. And just like that, you nod and find yourself in the pressure cooker of a game show hot seat. With family dynamics, setting boundaries is an issue one has to take seriously. The close ties and shared history can make it feel like you're walking a tightrope. One wrong move and you could disrupt the delicate balance of familial harmony.

Most especially in radical cultures, family loyalty and sacrifice are foregrounded in many families where cultural expectations blur individual boundaries. This can also make you feel like it's a tug of war: respect for family traditions and yet the urge to break free and assert your identity. The generational gap makes things worse. Maybe Grandma doesn't understand why you need "me time" because she reared eight kids without hearing of such a term. These boundary perception gaps can make limit-setting with family a minefield of emotions to navigate.

But fear not, for there are ways to communicate your needs clearly and respectfully within family dynamics. Consider initiating family meetings to discuss boundaries. It doesn't have to be that formal; think of it more like a dinner where everyone can share what they need. Open communication can lead to understanding and respect. Another effective strategy involves the use of "I feel" statements. Instead, say, "You never give me space," say, "I feel overwhelmed when I don't have time to myself." That helps to avoid sounding accusatory and invites a collaborative conversation.

Of course, setting boundaries with family can lead to pushback. Aunt Mildred might not take kindly to your newfound assertiveness, and Uncle Joe might think you're just being difficult. The key is to reassure them of your continued love and commitment. You are not shutting them out but making space for your needs. Let them know that respecting one another's boundaries is a great way to love one another, much in the same respect as Grandma's rule not to feed the dog at the table. A love-assertiveness balance can hold a boundary when resisted.

Healthy family boundaries are part of having more nurturing, more respectful relationships. Consider if a family communicates all their needs with respect. Communication will improve as people feel more comfortable sharing their thoughts and ideas without fearing judgment. Such conditions bring respect and understanding among the members, leading to a closer relationship. With well-defined boundaries, family time will be productive, considering the space and time for each member are respected. Like a correct seasoning in a family dish, it cannot overpower and ruin the flavors; therefore, the taste is excellent.

4.2 Interactive Element: Reflect on Family Boundaries

Take a moment to reflect on your family dynamics. Are there areas where your boundaries could be strengthened? Write down specific situations where you experienced discomfort or frustration. Consider how you might express your needs using "I feel" statements. Plan a casual family discussion to share your thoughts and encourage open dialogue. This exercise can help you approach family boundary-setting clearly and confidently, creating healthier relationships.

4.3 Setting Limits with Friends

Friendships are a lot like a dance: it takes balance and respect for both partners to keep the rhythm smooth. As it may seem that boundaries have no place in such relationships, they are crucial to maintaining harmony within them. Without limits, friendships can quickly become emotional burnout, leaving you to feel like the life raft in a sea of someone else's problems. You may be on call and able to drop everything in a moment while your needs meander into the distance. Boundaries keep you available for your friends without compromising yourself, so it's a space where both friends can breathe and grow.

Setting boundaries with your friends doesn't have to feel like the bearer of bad news. It is like setting the stage for a more honest and enriching connection. A simple strategy is to schedule regular catch-ups, preventing overcommitment and ensuring you both have time for other priorities. It's like penciling in an appointment for self-care, allowing you to maintain the friendship without becoming overwhelming. Another approach is to discuss preferences openly. Share that while you love spontaneous adventures, you also value downtime. It's all about finding that balance that works for both of you, like turning the volume up or down on a stereo. Sometimes, it's loud; sometimes, a softer tune will do.

But what if a friend continues to step across the lines in the sand? That is where an honest conversation needs to take place. Approach the situation empathetically and understand their perspective, yet clearly state your needs. You could say, "I appreciate our friendship; still, I would say that when I need some space, it doesn't feel like that's always respected. Can we work on that together?" That opens the door to understanding and collaboration rather than confrontation. Set consequences for boundary violations when necessary. Suppose one friend continually does not respect your needs. In that case, it may be time to re-evaluate to what extent both are involved in each other's lives, like determining which plants in your garden need more sun and which need to be pruned back.

Nurturing friendships that respect boundaries offers numerous benefits. Imagine a friendship based on a foundation of trust and mutual respect in which both individuals feel seen and understood by one another. This foundation creates a no-pressure situation that consequently will give way to blooming. You would build a relationship where both parties respect each other's boundaries, and it would be as strong as a ship that would survive stormy weather. Increased trust is the anchor that holds you steady, ensuring the friendship doesn't become one source of stress but rather a source of continued joy and support. Boundaries are not barriers but bridges to deeper connections, allowing both friends to be themselves without fearing judgment or rejection.

At the core, friendship has that partner in crime, having someone with your back, and vice versa. And by embracing boundaries, you ensure this partnership is balanced and respectful. It's about creating a space where both friends are heard and valued, the give-and-take is equal, and the relationship can thrive rather than one person being drained. Boundaries are the unsung heroes that make healthy friendships possible, providing the structure for both people to feel supported and understood. By setting them, you look after your well-being and strengthen the quality of the relationship to make it a strength and a source of joy for you and your friend.

4.4 Navigating Romantic Relationships

In the turning kaleidoscope of romantic relationships, boundaries often play an unsung hero in maintaining health and longevity for the partnerships. Imagine a relationship without boundaries-just like dancing with two people stepping on each other's toes. Boundaries are the choreography that keeps the dance smooth and enjoyable. They help preserve individuality, wherein each partner retains a sense of self within the relationship. Imagine a couple in which both partners have their hobbies and interests. Such individuality brings life into the partnership, whereby each person can get different experiences. It is like two flavors in one dish that complements and does not overpower. It is equally important to balance shared activities with personal time. While time spent together cements the bond between two people, personal time allows both individuals to reflect and grow. This balance between the two is what makes a relationship complete.

Setting boundaries with a romantic partner can be just as uncomfortable as a first date, but it's worth the misstep. It's always better to set expectations rather than work out misunderstandings later. Picture yourself sitting with your partner and discussing personal space, communication styles, and time management. In many ways, these conversations are like putting together a jigsaw puzzle- the bigger picture of your relationship comes into view. And check-ins about comfort levels are essential regularly. Relationships change, and boundaries change. A casual coffee chat about what is and isn't working can clear any gray areas. It's like a tune-up for your relationship, ensuring everything runs smoothly. These open dialogues foster trust and understanding, strengthening the foundation of your partnership.

Of course, no relationship is without its hiccups. Boundary conflicts can arise, often fueled by emotions like jealousy and trust issues. Imagine finding yourself in a situation where your partner feels insecure about your close friendship with someone else. These feelings are normal yet need to be aired. Talking through the root of such insecurities and ways of reassuring one another will help avoid the danger of bitterness setting in. Another potential minefield involves finances. Clear communication is vital, from who pays for dinner to how joint expenses will be divided. Imagine having to decide on financial goals and responsibilities with your partner. This transparency helps clear misunderstandings and keeps the relationship on an even keel. Recognition and understanding are probably what romantic relationships are cemented with. One of the substantial ways of addressing boundary needs with empathy is to listen to respond. Imagine, for instance, that your partner is concerned about feeling overlooked; instead of jumping to conclusions or going on the defensive, you listen closely and acknowledge the feelings. This simple act shows that you value their perspective, even if it differs from yours. It's like wrapping a warm blanket around your partner, offering comfort and reassurance. By approaching boundary discussions with empathy, you create a safe space for honest communication, ensuring both partners feel heard and valued. This respect lays the groundwork for a resilient partnership capable of weathering any storm that comes its way.

4.5 Professional Boundaries within the Workplace

Coming into the workplace without boundaries is like a busy city without a map. The need for boundaries at work cannot be talked about enough. They are guardrails to keep professionalism intact and maintain the right work-life balance. Establishing these limits is essential to avoid burnout in a world where emails and messages can reach you anytime, day or night. Imagine being always on, responding to challenges at work, even during dinner with your family. It may seem like dedication, but it will undoubtedly lead to burnout. In this case, boundaries are the shield that protects your energy so that you can give your best without running empty.

To set professional boundaries effectively, start by establishing precise work hours. It's like having a closing time for the shop; when the clock strikes, the shutters go down. Communicate such hours to colleagues and supervisors about when you're available and when not. This cushions them, so they know not to expect anything from those particular hours since those are your personal hours. Another strategy is to delegate appropriately. If your workload resembles a

Jenga tower about to topple, it is time to reassess which blocks you can pass on. Delegation lightens your load and empowers others, fostering a collaborative environment. It's like sharing the spotlight in a play, allowing everyone to shine.

Despite our best efforts, boundary violations can occur. Handling them with professionalism is key. Documenting interactions is a practical step. It's like keeping a diary of events, noting instances where boundaries may have been ignored. This record will be priceless if the issue needs to be resolved with formality. In the case of a persistent boundary breach, one can always seek further support from HR. There, they function as mediators in the workplace drama, ensuring that boundaries are maintained and respect is conveyed accordingly. Consider the HR as the referee in a game, ensuring everybody plays the game within the rules of the game without overstepping the line.

A respect-for-boundary workplace culture is where productivity and morale are grown. It is like a well-oiled machine where each part knows its place and functions well. Employees who feel that their boundaries are respected will likely perform best. There is an increase in job satisfaction because individuals feel valued and understood. This respect creates a positive atmosphere that enhances collaboration and minimizes conflict. It's like an orchestra, all playing different instruments to play a beautiful symphony. It all starts at the top; it begins with you setting an example yourself. By respecting people's boundaries, you set an example for others to be respectful toward them, too.

Setting up a boundary-respective environment is not an individual success but a collective success. Where the boundaries are respected, so is the mutual respect and trust. People feel empowered to speak about their needs because they can be confident their concerns will be heard and valued. A feeling of empowerment fosters increased engagement and a sense of ownership. A question is whether one wants a garden that smothers its plants or sets them free to grow and bloom. This could be where creativity and innovation can occur, unhindered by the weight of overcommitting and associated stress with blurred lines.

4.6 Visual Element: Boundary Reminder Chart

Create a Boundary Reminder Chart for your workspace. This could be a visual of your work hours, key tasks, and delegation points. Place it somewhere visible to remind yourself and others of your boundaries. It's a daily reminder to keep your commitments to yourself and your work and stay balanced to continue being productive and energized.

4.7 Boundaries in Digital and Social Media Spaces

In this digital world, a different kind of challenge arises when trying to set boundaries online. Unlike the real world, this one is always on, careening along with the relentless momentum of perpetual readiness. Like your buzzing phone- a swarm of bees, notifications light up and demand action 24/7. It puts pressure on an individual, and one feels that they are on call for anyone, from a friend to a distant acquaintance; this contributes to digital exhaustion. It's a feeling that the world expects you to be on tap at any moment, which utterly confuses the boundary between personal time and screen time. This rapidly leads to burnout in cases where the expectation is always to be online, for one would think of a hamster running on a wheel and never being able to step off this digital treadmill.

Privacy concerns make setting digital boundaries complicated. In a day and age when oversharing is only a click away, it is easy to forget that everything must not be transmitted to your entire social network. Sharing every meal, mood, and musing can leave you feeling exposed, like living in a glass house. The more you share, the more vulnerable you become to cyberbullying and negative interactions. These digital boundary violations can create emotional distress as harsh words and unsolicited opinions seep into your consciousness. Hiding behind the internet can bring out the worst in people, leading to a virtual minefield of negativity. Cyberbullying can leave permanent scars and affect your mental health and self-esteem. It is like inviting strangers into the living room and asking them to judge your taste in decoration.

Considering such challenges, setting digital boundaries becomes imperative. Start by regulating your screen time as you would do with your favorite snack to avoid overindulgence. Set times to go on social media and check your emails to give your brain a rest. The aware disconnection, however, places an intervening zone between you and the digital world for a reason to breathe. Another powerful mechanism involves facilitating adjusted privacy settings regarding social networking. This is like changing the curtains in your virtual house to be able to manage who sees inside. In editing your online output, you're giving yourself a safe place to go where you can be yourself without fear of judgment or intrusion.

Mindful digital engagement is using technology deliberately, not being controlled by it. As one might do in an art gallery, take a moment to curate your social media feeds. Following accounts that align with your social needs brings joy instead of stress. Be selective with your interactions, choosing quality over quantity. Sometimes, engaging with a few meaningful posts can be more fulfilling than scrolling through endless updates. This is an intentional way to build resilience that will enable you to confidently and clearly navigate the digital world.

Setting and maintaining digital boundaries empowers you to control your online experience. You can think of your digital space as a cultivated garden, carefully nurtured to nurture what you want and weed out everything else. Conscious curation creates a balance and allows you to enjoy technology without falling prey to its vices. This way, digital boundaries become a form of self-care, ensuring your well-being does not take a hit due to virtual interaction.

4.8 Handling Boundary Violations in Relationships

Relationships, whether friendships, family relationships, or partnerships, are much like playing Jenga: when everybody respects one another's boundaries, the tower goes up strong, but if your expressed wishes or emotional boundaries are crossed, then it's as though he reached in and pulled out a block that wasn't supposed to be pulled-the whole thing starts to wobble. A boundary violation is when someone does not respect your limits, intentionally or otherwise. This may be continuing to discuss a topic you have made off-limits or making decisions regarding you without your consent. Emotional boundary overstepping can include manipulation or invalidating your feelings. It's like someone barging into your personal space without knocking, leaving you vulnerable and exposed.

Boundary violations require courage and clarity to address. The best approach is direct communication. First, declare how the violation affected you. Consider a scenario: "When you shared my private thoughts with them, I felt betrayed. I need to know that my privacy is respected." The key here is to focus on your feelings and the impact rather than accusing the other person. Using this method keeps dialogues productive rather than confrontational.

It also sets the stage for what will occur if this boundary is crossed again. It may sound like, "If this happens again, I must reconsider how much I share with you." These consequences do not punish the other person but protect your emotional well-being. Think of setting up guardrails to prevent future breaches.

Breaches of boundaries can leave emotional scars that remain long after the incident initially occurred. Trust, once breached, takes more time and forbearance to reconstruct. You could even feel so betrayed like the carpet has been yanked from underneath your feet. This feeling of disempowerment is likely to lower your self-confidence and make you feel less worthy within the relationship. It feels like finally knowing that a vital ally has become an enemy you have trusted and relied on to support you in times of need. These feelings are real and should be validated. They tend to snowball into how you relate to the violator and others. Violations can be harmful, yet they are also an opportunity to understand and grow if treated with mindfulness and care.

Rebuilding trust in people around you after a boundary violation is a sensitive process. It requires open and honest dialogue from both parties, much like mending a cracked vase with patience and precision. Start by acknowledging the violation and expressing your willingness to move forward. Encourage the other person to share their perspective and listen actively to their response. It's like opening the lines of communication and ensuring they remain clear. This dialogue will help both parties understand what went wrong and how to prevent it from happening again. It's about finding common ground and re-establishing the boundaries that were previously crossed. This process involves healing and reinforcing the relationship with more substantial, resilient bonds.

It is a process and not an event. The boundaries will continue to change, just as relationships do. You protect yourself and allow for healthier relationships by talking openly about what was violated and doing so with feeling. That's how you ensure your relationships stay supportive and respectful so they can thrive. Let's look now at how these apply in various life contexts to ensure your boundaries are respected.

Chapter Five

Mindfulness and Self-Reflection Exercises

Visualize the following: You're in a busy café, trying to enjoy a latte, but all you can hear is conversations and the hiss of an espresso machine. Your mind is filled with to-do lists and worries. The noise of life often drowns out the quiet voice of your needs and boundaries. But what if you could turn down the volume and tune into a more transparent channel? Enter mindfulness- a practice as ancient as it is effective. Mindfulness offers a way to be present, quiet the mental chatter, and focus on what truly matters: understanding and respecting your boundaries.

Mindfulness isn't about sitting cross-legged on some mountaintop and finding enlightenment. It's simply awareness of the present moment without judgment. Such awareness of yourself then becomes relevant in understanding your needs for boundaries. Through mindfulness practices, you are better aware of when your boundaries have been stretched or how overwhelmed you may feel. Imagine being able to catch yourself before you agree to something you would not want to, merely out of your increased emotional and physical self-awareness; this could mark the beginning of establishing and preserving healthy boundaries.

Mindful breathing is one of the most effective practices. It's like a pause in the world around you. Find a quiet place, sit comfortably, and close your eyes. Begin by taking deep breaths and concentrate on the feeling of the air going in and going out of your body. As thoughts inevitably drift in, acknowledge them, then gently redirect your focus to your breath. This exercise helps create a mental space to assess your needs and boundaries without the usual noise. It's a moment of tranquility in a world that rarely stops for breath.

Another practice is the body scan exercise. Think of it as a full-body check-in, where you give each part of your body a little attention. Lie down or sit, and close your eyes. Start from your toes, magnetically moving to the crown of your head, noting any tense or uncomfortable parts of the body. As you scan, breathe into those areas and exhale tension. The exercise grounds you in the present moment. It helps you become more attuned to physical signals indicating stress or boundary violations. It's like giving your body a chance to speak, a chance it rarely gets in this crazy world.

Mindfulness and clarity go together. Being present means that you are much clearer on your needs for boundaries. For example, consider your emotional reactions in an argument: it might help you understand where you need to draw the line. You sense a tightening of your chest when a friend expects too much from you. This immediately suggests where to set a limit. Being present allows you to recognize the signs and respond thoughtfully rather than impulsively.

Applying mindfulness to your daily routines might simply be practicing a walking meditation. Take a walk, noticing how your feet strike the ground with each step. Create a rhythm in how you walk, and feel the breeze on your skin as you do so. When your mind wanders, gently bring it back to your walking. It develops awareness, like meditation in motion, and lets you keep a calm, focused mind.

The profound long-term benefits of mindfulness include how the boundaries stay consistent with regular practice. Mindfulness helps to decrease stress and anxiety, which enables you to approach whatever situation comes your way with clarity and a steady heart. It's as though you wear a personal compass oriented toward your values and needs. Mindfulness can, over time, change how one relates to the world and make one more resilient during life's ups and downs.

5.2 Interactive Element: Mindfulness Routine Checklist

Create a Mindfulness Routine Checklist. In the checklist below, write three mindfulness practices you want to try this week: mindful breathing, a body scan, and walking meditation. Check them off as you complete each one. Reflect on any changes you notice in your awareness and boundary clarity. Keep this checklist visible to remind yourself of your commitment to mindfulness.

5.3 Journaling Prompts for Self-Discovery

Imagine each day being a day when moments become lessons to know oneself better. Journaling can be the bridge to self-discovery, the tool for trying to understand and understand your needs for setting boundaries. Let this be in your mind as a talking-with-your-inside thing you can unpack daily without interruptions. When you write down your thoughts and feelings about daily interactions, you develop insights that otherwise slip through memory cracks. It's as if a personal detective is uncovering clues about what makes you tick. Each entry becomes a snapshot of your emotional landscape, showing patterns and preferences in interacting with the world.

Begin by considering some guiding questions. "What boundaries did I uphold today?" is an excellent starting point. This question allows you to reflect on when you may have stood your ground in some situation where it was so easy to cave in. You could have said no to an extra task at work or excused yourself from attending a social event you did not want to attend. Knowing these little victories, you know that you can keep your boundaries. Another prompt to consider is, "How did I feel when somebody respected my boundaries?" This question helps you tune into the emotional rewards of boundary-setting, reinforcing the positive feelings associated with being true to yourself. Regularly engaging with these prompts creates a roadmap of your boundary experiences, highlighting areas where you excel and those needing more attention.

Journaling does more than document your thoughts. It's a tool for personal growth- a window to an ever-evolving you. Every entry serves as a mirror to your inner world, carrying with it much insight into the emotional resonance inside you. You may observe in writing how themes or circumstances keep reoccurring to test your boundaries in every situation. Awareness will then provide a step toward making a change: finding those areas of your life where you need to set stronger willpower. These reflections will help you realize your needs and voice them louder in due time. Peeling layers off an onion to get to your core, layer after layer, entry by entry.

Of course, journaling does not have to be restricted to conventional writing. It can get a bit creative to make self-expression even deeper and different. Bullet journaling might be used to keep track visually. Make lists of boundary goals or track your progress with colorful charts. This method gets your logical brain involved and adds a splash of creativity to the process. Visual journaling is another unique approach. Sketch your feelings or create collages that represent your boundary experiences. These artistic expressions capture emotions words might miss, providing a rich tapestry of self-discovery.

Journaling is the journey of discovery that invites a person into the depths of introspection and creativity. The practice entails regularly recording boundary experiences and delving into the reasons behind such decisions. Such a habit builds in a person a sense of self-awareness in daily life. It empowers them to approach boundary-setting with clarity and confidence. Journaling will become the trusted source, be it through writing or art, in your search to understand and respect your boundaries.

5.4 Reflecting on Past Boundary Experiences

Visualize your life as a collection of snapshots, each at that one moment when you tried to set a boundary. Some of these pictures might be blurry, where the lines weren't clear, while others are sharp, capturing a victory where you stood firm. It reflects those experiences, a look back in the album not to live in the past but to learn from it. Looking back at these instances, you start to observe your pattern of attempts to set boundaries. Maybe there's one repetitive theme where you always say yes to your family's demands, even when it stretches you too thin. Alternatively, you might find that there is one area of avoidance in which you rarely say no to friends, even if you need some downtime. Recognizing these patterns is the first step in understanding where your boundaries have succeeded and where they could use a little reinforcement.

Reflection isn't about playing the blame game with yourself. Instead, approach it as a curious detective piecing together a puzzle. Consider asking yourself, "What were the outcomes of past boundary attempts?" Think about situations where your boundaries were respected and how that felt. Was the effect greater self-respect or closer intimacy? Conversely, think about times when you did not set limits. What happened? Did you become stressed or resentful? Knowing these repercussions helps you to better understand what boundary setting has done in your life. It's like looking through a magnifying glass, making your actions' effects more apparent.

Another question would be, "What could I have done differently?" It's not an exercise in self-criticism but one of considering alternatives that could have been taken. For example, if trying to set a boundary previously resulted in resistance, reflect on how you might have better communicated. Perhaps using more assertive language or another time to address the issue might have made a difference. This reflective process is like a play rehearsal: you improve with every run. Contemplating various strategies arms you with choices for future boundary-setting efforts.

Learning from the past is one of the most effective ways to inform your future actions. It aids one in viewing backward and understanding what has and has not worked for you. Recognizing successful tactics helps you build on them, creating a strong foundation for future boundary-setting. It's like discovering a recipe that works and tweaking it to perfection. At the same time, understanding what didn't work allows you to avoid repeating mistakes. This knowledge empowers you to approach boundary-setting with more confidence and precision.

Approach this reflection with compassion and understanding. Past mistakes are part of being human; everyone wants to redo moments. Accepting these missteps without judgment is crucial to growth. Think of it as hugging yourself, acknowledging that you're doing your best. Embracing a nonjudgmental mindset creates a safe space for honest introspection. This acceptance fosters a sense of self-compassion, enabling you to move forward without the weight of regret.

So, in reflecting on those past boundary experiences, remember that this is not about perfection; it is about progress and learning to handle your boundaries more skillfully. Whether you flip through those mental snapshots or rehearse new strategies, every step brings you closer to an empowered, more self-aware you.

5.5 Meditation Techniques for Emotional Balance

Think of your feelings as the rush-hour subway, full of energy pushing and shoving. Every thought is another passenger clamoring for attention. Meditation is getting off that crowded train and going out into a quiet platform, from which you may observe the mess if you choose to. This is a technique for emotional balancing, an anchor to turbulence. Setting boundaries with regular meditation can be a potent ally in ensuring clarity and calm when stress is in action.

Some meditations are guided and, therefore, can bring relaxation and clarity of mind into the state. Close your eyes and imagine yourself in some peaceful landscape: maybe a sunny meadow or next to some quiet stream. You hear the soothing voice that will help you concentrate your thoughts and relax your body. Such practice soothes the mind and sharpens your perception of personal needs and limits. Relaxed and centered, you're apt to notice more when a boundary is being nudged or breached. Your mind observes the world and makes decisions with clarity and poise. Guided meditation acts as a personal tour guide through the maze of your emotions to keep you in balance.

A concrete yet particular meditation technique that promotes emotional wellness is loving-kindness meditation. It includes focusing your mind on the feeling of love and compassion towards yourself and others. Sit comfortably, close your eyes, and imagine sending warmth and kindness to yourself, repeating specific phrases, such as, "May I be happy, may I be safe." Gradually extend these wishes to loved ones, acquaintances, and even those you find challenging. This meditation nurtures connectedness and empathy, which in turn will improve your emotional resilience. In developing compassion, you provide protection against negativity that will help you set boundaries with grace and understanding. It's like wrapping yourself in a warm blanket of goodwill, protecting against cold winds of judgment and criticism.

The effects of meditation on emotional health are potent. Regular practitioners often report heightened emotional resilience, akin to having an emotional shock absorber. When life throws you a curveball, meditation helps you bounce back more quickly, with less time spent in emotional turmoil. This resilience is particularly helpful in setting boundaries because it gives you the strength to stand firm in the face of pushback or discomfort. Meditation teaches your mind to stay balanced, as would an experienced tightrope walker, even in the most challenging circumstances.

Needless to say, meditation can be integrated into daily routines without having to give up worldly goods and join a monastery. It can be smoothly fitted into your daily life, like that comforting thread sewn into the seams of your routine. Consider starting your day with a morning meditation ritual. Spend only five to ten minutes in the morning. Find a quiet place, sit comfortably, and focus on your breath or some simple mantra. This sets a positive tone for the day, grounding you before the chaos begins. It's like putting on emotional armor, ready to tackle whatever the day might bring.

Work breaks can be beneficial, too. Take a few-minute meditating break when your stress level rises or you lose concentration. Shut your office door, eliminate distractions, and focus on breathing or soothing visualization. These brief moments of meditation reset and renew your mind, preparing it for renewed focus. They are like an oasis in a desert, able to return to tasks with renewed vigor and clarity.

Setting a regular meditation practice is like adding regular oil changes to your mind and spirit. They keep you running smoothly, reducing emotional wear and tear. By prioritizing meditation, you create space for yourself, a place where you can recharge and reaffirm your boundaries. It's not about escaping from the world but engaging with it more fully, with a calm mind and an open heart.

5.6 Mindful Communication Skills

Imagine you're attending an event, surrounded by conversations, like in a garden full of bees. In these situations, being present may be far from your reality. However, mindfulness in communication helps to clearly set up the boundaries and understanding required. It means paying attention to the person across from you rather than the ping of your phone or the grocery list running through your head. This presence turns a simple exchange into a meaningful dialogue. When you truly listen, you hear more than words-you catch the subtlety of tone and emotion, the unspoken clues that reveal what's being said. It's like tuning into a radio frequency that captures every nuance, making the conversation more prosperous and transparent.

Being present to listen is a big part of mindful communication. It involves more than simply nodding while planning what you might say next. Visualize yourself as a detective who intently observes the speaker's body language, tone of voice, and choice of words. This degree of attention tells the speaker that their view is valued and can build mutual respect between two people. As part of active listening, paraphrase another person's words before responding. This might feel a little weird at first, like learning a new step in dancing, but it reassures them that you get their perspective. This little trick can avoid misunderstandings, turning conflicts into contact opportunities.

The advantages of mindful communication do not stop at the reduction of misunderstandings. The ripples flow into every sphere of life as relationships and respect grow. Being fully present sends a message of sincerity and empathy, and this naturally begets clearer boundary exchanges. Suppose a friend asked you for a favor that put you out of your comfort zone. Besides a straight-out no, mindful communication would cause the pause, a considered response to their request. Your response is balanced to the needs of another, and that is where a relationship thrives. Mindful communication is not all about the no; it's more like, "I hear you, and here's how I can help."

Role-playing can be an excellent way to hone in on these skills. Think of it as a rehearsal for life's unpredictable conversations. You can role-play with a friend, taking turns practicing mindful listening and boundary-setting. One might express a concern, while the other practices active listening, summarizing, and reflecting on the key points. This exercise builds confidence and skill, preparing you for real-world interactions. It's a rehearsal, so to speak, for the opening night. Through practice, you develop empathy by listening, which shifts your perspective. Communication becomes more affluent, and you understand things better.

It means mindful communication turns the mundane-regular interaction into an opportunity for growth and connecting. The beauty of such communication is that it helps address complex human relationships with an open-heart and much surety of hand. As you master these skills, your conversations have depth, and boundaries begin to hold respect. Mindfulness is not a magic wand, meaning communication would become impeccable. Yet, it does serve as a guide toward more genuine and compassionate interchanges.

5.7 Constant Reevaluation and Readjustment

Think of taking a road trip without a map or GPS. You may know where you're going, but how would you know you're on the right track or if you need to stop off anywhere? In this way, regular self-assessment works like a great Global Positioning System for your boundaries. Constantly checking in with yourself helps ensure that your boundaries work. These are routines for check-ins, likened to pit stops where one ascertains what is working and what needs a tweak. Perhaps it is those few minutes in the morning over coffee when you reflect on whether yesterday's boundaries served you well or in the evening wind-down, reflecting on the moments that had you feeling stretched too thin. These moments of reflection are invaluable opportunities to recalibrate and ensure your boundaries align with your current needs.

To help you with this ongoing evaluation, consider using boundary assessment worksheets. These are not mere sheets of paper but mirrors reflecting your boundary landscape. They allow you to identify areas where you thrive and those needing reinforcement. Picture a worksheet with columns for different aspects of your life—work, relationships, personal time—where you can rate your satisfaction with your boundaries. Fill these out regularly, maybe monthly, to track your progress and uncover patterns. This structured approach not only highlights areas needing attention but also celebrates where you're excelling. It is like a report card for personal growth, in which you get concrete insight into how well your boundaries work. Within every assessment, you get clarity on how to shape the boundary into something that works best for you and your changing needs.

Now, flexibility within this recipe of setting boundaries is the magic ingredient. Life is dynamic; it keeps changing with experiences and challenges. Consider that, in the same way, you change clothes for the seasons, so must boundaries change according to life's seasons. Flexibility means knowing that what worked for you last year no longer serves you now. The new job asks for firmer time boundaries, while the developing friendship asks for open emotional boundaries. You will only keep your boundaries relevant and practical by being open to change. It's about being willing to tweak and adjust without feeling like you're losing ground. This adaptability is not a sign of weakness but strength, showing a deep understanding of your evolving self.

The benefits of continual adaptation are profound. As you align your boundaries with your personal growth, they become less like rigid walls and more like a supportive framework. This alignment will ensure that your boundaries support your goals and aspirations, not work against them. Just as a gardener would regularly prune and nurture each of his plants to full bloom, your boundaries also need this regular attention to flourish. By adjusting them, you are creating space to grow and thrive while being unhindered by outdated limitations. The whole self-engagement through reassessment and readjustments allows you to live more authentically and for your boundaries to reflect that true self.

Continued self-assessment and adjustment are needed to keep a dialogue going with yourself. This conversation about where you've been going, are going, and currently going is based on an active practice: one of regular check-in, some tools of assessment, and flexibility that creates effective, thereby empowering, boundaries. Your boundaries become alive and real and change with you as you walk your path. In embracing this process continuously, you will realize that your boundaries are not lines in the sand but supportive structures guiding you toward a more fulfilling life of balance.

As we conclude, remember that boundaries are dynamic; they grow and evolve to support you, not restrict or confine you. In the next segment, we will understand how to apply adaptable boundaries in everyday life, both personal and professional.

Chapter Six

Conflict Resolution and Negotiation Strategies

Imagine sitting with your friend, having a casual conversation, when, out of the blue, an unexpected comment strikes you like a rogue wave. The atmosphere in the room is tense, and what started as a simple conversation has escalated into a full-blown conflict. Well, don't worry because you are not alone! Conflict is as natural as breathing, especially in relationships where diverse personalities and perspectives collide. It's like putting hot sauce on your favorite food. Too much can burn your mouth out, but a little can spice things up. The nature of the conflict must be understood to enable one to sail through these stormy waters without being pulled under by the torrent.

Conflict arises mainly because of miscommunication and misunderstanding, the arch-nemesis of peace. It's a kind of telephone game: the less the message is repeated, the more distorted it becomes. Misunderstandings make even the most trivial conversations become battles. Sometimes, it's because of one misused word or an imagined tone of voice. Conflicts are also nourished by the differences in values and expectations. You may be wearing rose-colored glasses, whereas your friend insists on seeing reality with no-nonsense eyeglasses. The reason is straightforward: such differences may bring up friction because people hang on to their beliefs, as would a cat on a sunny windowsill. This awareness can better arm you to handle conflicts with empathy and understanding instead of building resentment.

Understanding common patterns in conflict can prevent you from being caught up in the vicious circle of arguments. One such pattern is escalation cycles, wherein a minor disagreement escalates into a full-blown shouting match. Like a snowball going down a hill, it picks up mass and speed and then crashes into some unsuspecting village. The process of conflict escalation does much the same if left to fester. A minor issue can escalate out of proportion when emotions and tempers flare. Noticing these patterns allows you to intervene early and stop the snowball before it causes damage to your relationships. By recognizing these cycles, you can stop, take a deep breath, and get the conversation back into peaceful waters.

How we perceive things and our emotions, play a significant role in shaping conflict dynamics. Stress and emotional triggers are like matchsticks-they can turn even the tiniest spark of disagreement into a flame. Just think of getting up on the wrong side of the bed, and everything seems to bother you. Stressors impact perception because a neutral comment can be perceived as an attack. Understanding these psychological aspects helps people manage their emotions and approach conflicts with a level head. By acknowledging your stressors, you can defuse tension and communicate more effectively, turning potential conflicts into opportunities for growth.

Conflict comes in many flavors, each requiring a unique approach. Task conflicts revolve around disagreements related to tasks or responsibilities, like deciding who should take out the trash or lead a group project. They're often straightforward and can be resolved through clear communication and compromise. Relationship conflicts, on the other hand, involve deeper issues, such as values, trust, or emotional needs. These are more complicated conflicts that may call for a much subtler approach. Think of your relationship issues like a ball of yarn tangled and knotted, each strand representing one aspect of your relationship. These things take time to untangle, but with empathy and understanding, a resolution can be reached to strengthen your connection.

6.2 Interactive Element: Conflict Reflection Exercise

Take a moment to reflect on a recent conflict you have experienced. What were the root causes? Was it a task or relationship conflict? Identify what emotions and perceptions drove your response. Write thoughts in a journal, including any patterns or hot spots you noticed. How might you handle similar situations in the future? The exercise builds self-awareness, devises ways to manage conflict effectively, and turns it into opportunities for growth and understanding.

SETTING BOUNDARIES

6.3 Strategies for Peaceful Negotiation

Consider negotiation a dance where two parties move harmoniously to reach a mutually beneficial agreement. It's not about winning or losing but finding a rhythm that works for everyone. Negotiation serves as a bridge in relationships, connecting different perspectives and desires. The key to knowing who takes the trash out or how to balance holiday visits between families is negotiation. It involves a process where both parties converse with each other and show a willingness to understand the needs of others. The bargaining tool can turn arguments into opportunities for growth and deeper connections.

Preparation is your secret weapon. It's like packing for a trip: having an extra pair of socks is better than being caught in the rain barefoot. Before entering negotiations, take time to understand what you want to achieve. Firm your objectives and determine which boundaries you're willing to flex and which are non-negotiable. You are a detective gathering clues about your needs and the other party's interests. This prepares a focused discussion to keep you on target when emotions surge. Knowing what you want and where you stand provides a strong platform to enter into negotiations, prepared for the highs and lows of conversations.

Setting clear objectives and boundaries is like having a map of unfamiliar territory. It leads you, so you will not veer off course. While negotiating, express your goals clearly and any limits you must maintain. The transparency will establish trust because you're not hiding something behind your back. If you are trying to negotiate the household chores with your roommate, state your availability and willingness to compromise from the start. This openness reduces the risk of misunderstandings and lays a solid foundation for your productive dialogue. You make safety for both parties to state their needs and work toward a satisfying resolution by articulating your objectives and boundaries.

Empathy is the star of negotiation, which can turn what might be a tug-of-war into a cooperative effort. You step into the other party's shoes and try to understand their perspective, much like a detective putting together the pieces of a mystery. Active empathy exercises can help you practice this skill. For a second, try to put yourself in the other party's shoes: What could they possibly want to receive from this negotiation? You can then tailor your approach to their needs and advocate for your own. Empathy will make them feel the negotiation is a dialogue, not a monologue, where both parties are heard and understood.

Common ground is what any successful negotiation is based upon. That means making a bridge where both parties have something to add and complete. Search for common ground or goals where an agreement can be based on a solid foundation. Brainstorming works well here because brainstorming fosters creative options that will aid in finding mutual benefit. For instance, you're planning a vacation with your partner. You may have different ideas about the itinerary, but both want a relaxing and enjoyable trip. By identifying this shared goal, you can explore options and compromises that satisfy both of you. Where there is common ground, there is usually collaboration. Where there is collaboration, the door opens for a win-win outcome where both leave the negotiation valued and satisfied.

6.4 Compromise Without Compelling Yourself

Compromise gets a bad rap because it often invokes images of losing ground or giving in. The healthy compromise, though, is an exercise in win-win scenarios, where both parties go away feeling valued. Think of two artists working together on a mural; each brings his own colors, style, and outcomes, a work that neither could do alone. Compromise in a relationship should not be seen as sacrificing personal values on an altar of appeasement. Instead, it integrates perceptions, much like a well-performed duet. The secret lies in the line separating healthy compromise from core belief sacrifice. Suppose you constantly compromise on what is important to you and others. In that case, it might be time for reevaluation. Compromise is about give-and-take, not losing out.

A compromise involves clarity regarding non-negotiables. Think of these as the foundation stones of a building; take them away, and the whole structure will shake. Knowing what you cannot give up helps you navigate discussions clearly and confidently. Before you compromise, take a moment to reflect on what truly matters: holding on to family traditions, alone time, or professional ethics. Defining these non-negotiables gives you a sure base from which to negotiate. This clarity allows you to go into the discussion with an open mind and explore possibilities, yet be true to your core.

It is in compromising that integrity needs to be maintained. It is like a tightrope, balancing between solutions and staying true to self. Personal value assessments might help you balance this tightrope. Check in with yourself: Is this compromise in line with my values?

Am I being true to myself? These questions will guide you through the negotiation process. Compromise doesn't mean giving up your beliefs; it is about finding creative solutions to satisfy your needs while considering others. Knowing where you stand, you can make compromises that don't make you sacrifice who you are to find common ground.

Compromise has its advantages, extending beyond resolving the conflict immediately. When carried out well, compromise in relationships fortifies them through cooperation and mutual understanding. It's like weaving a tapestry; each thread represents a different perspective. Together, these threads create a cohesive and beautiful whole.

Compromise involves openness in communication because both parties are engaged in finding a solution. This joint effort resolves the issue and opens up avenues for future interactions. Compromise makes relationships more viable because both parties feel their views have been considered. It creates an environment where people are willing to work together, knowing their needs and values are acknowledged.

In the light of this, compromise becomes a tool for building bridges, not walls. It helps you negotiate the complexities of a relationship with finesse and sensitivity. By embracing compromise without losing out on yourself, you create a space where dialogue thrives and connections deepen. It is an act of carving a familiar path on which each feels valued and supported. While compromising, remember it's not about losing or winning. It is the blending of perspectives in harmony that nurtures relationships and promotes incredible personal growth.

6.5 De-Escalation Techniques during Heated Moments

Imagine an argument with tension high enough in the air to cut it with a knife. Your heart is racing, your palms are sweaty, and you are literally one word away from a full-on emotional eruption. That is where de-escalation techniques come in, like some trusty extinguisher for the flames of conflict. De-escalation is not about winning or losing but calming the storm before it sweeps everything away. The power of calm responses cannot be overemphasized - they are life jackets in choppy waters that keep you afloat when emotions pull you under. When someone is yelling, responding with a level voice can be disarming. It is like whispering in a library; it's a game-changer in the vibe and ushers in quiet. Mastery of the skill can make what could have been a disaster into a manageable discussion.

Among the de-escalation techniques, pausing is simply one of the most potent. Sometimes, taking a break is the best medicine when emotions are riots. Even briefly, stepping away from the situation allows everyone involved to cool down. Just imagine hitting the pause button on a hot argument and going outside for some air; refreshing, like a cold splash on a scorching summer day. You suddenly get your thoughts together, find a calm space, and approach the situation clearly. Sometimes, you have to reboot that frozen computer. Another one of the most underrated de-escalation tools is humor. Used properly, it defuses tension and lightens the mood. Imagine a very tense standoff, and then suddenly, someone makes a light-hearted joke that cuts through the hostility. Laughter is a universal language that unites, making a resolution much easier.

Body language is critical in de-escalation. Open and relaxed postures make a statement of calm and openness. Visualize yourself in a defensive stance, arms across the chest, and furrowed brows. Now, imagine uncrossing those arms, relaxing your shoulders, and holding the gaze. These non-verbal signals would indicate that you are open to discourse, not wanting to fight. It's like opening a window to let fresh air in; suddenly, it is not so stifling. By being aware of one's body language, one can often create an arena where others can express themselves without fear of escalation.

Practice de-escalation skills through role-playing. Like in a play, the more you practice, the more natural it will become. First, brainstorm scenarios that might lead to conflict, then act them out with a partner. Practice modulating your tone, responding calmly, and using humor. Maybe you are negotiating over who gets the last slice of pizza - a very trivial situation, yet perfect for testing your de-escalation techniques. With these exercises, you will develop confidence in conflict management and turn probable fireworks into peaceful resolutions.

6.6 Building Mutual Respect Through Boundaries

Like fine-tuning instruments in an orchestra for excellent performance, this is what clear boundaries do in relationships: create a rhythm where trust and safety flourish. Boundaries are the sheet music on which the dance between people happens. When you set boundaries, the stage is set for respect to take center. In that sense, boundaries will tell people to respect yourself and wish others would do the same. That is a fertile ground where trust can sprout. It's not building walls; it's just setting guidelines to protect your well-being. This respect develops a feeling of security, where both parties feel assured that their needs and limits are comprehended and regarded.

In this regard, reinforcing respect for boundaries requires an ongoing process of reaffirmation in communication. It's like tuning your instrument before every performance. This frequent checking-in with oneself and others ensures clarity and respect for boundaries. Open conversations about boundaries can avoid misunderstandings and missteps. It would be as if there were a roadmap for the relationship, with everyone knowing the route and where the destination lies. Boundaries will be automatic; they are communicated repeatedly, and the chance of conflict will be minimal. That reinforces respect by showing that the bounds are not momentary hindrances but are part of the structure that holds the relationship together. Strong respect will surely last with transparency and consistency.

Boundaries are also protective measures against potential conflicts. Visualize them as trail signs: they point the way around things you don't want to fall into. The sooner one can set certain expectations, the easier it is to prevent a problem from escalating and becoming a more serious conflict. Thus, talking over the boundaries from the beginning allows clearing up what can be tolerated. This clarity eliminates most of those misunderstandings leading to disputes. Setting the boundary is like drawing a line in the sand, marking the limits of behavior and interaction. Setting those boundaries early creates a cushion that prevents unnecessary friction. Thus, the relationship can blossom without the looming specter of discord.

Building an environment of respect extends beyond individual boundaries. It requires developing a culture that celebrates shared boundaries and upholds them in honor. Imagine a neighborhood where everyone contributes to building a fence that serves all. The setting of boundaries together allows for dialogue and understanding. By allowing others to contribute to setting your boundaries, you allow them to take some ownership of responsibility. This shared approach will breed respect since everyone has a stake in maintaining the set limits. It is like having a team working in unison towards a common goal, and every member's opinions are considered. In this kind of environment, boundaries are not restrictive but empowering tools that elevate the quality of the relationship.

Establishing a respectful environment through shared boundaries involves active participation: holding open discussions where everyone can express their needs and concerns. Consider regular check-ins to review and adjust boundaries as necessary. This ongoing dialogue reinforces respect, showing that boundaries are neither unbending nor unyielding but susceptible to shift according to changing circumstances. It is like tending a garden; one must tend to it regularly so every plant can grow. By nurturing respect within this culture, a safe space is created wherein boundaries can be honored and celebrated. This respect, therefore, becomes the cornerstone of that relationship, where the bond between individuals tightens to enhance the quality of the relationship.

6.7 Growth Opportunities through Conflict Learning

Think of the conflict as a grumpy old neighbor complaining about your lawn. And yet, you learn something from him every time he comes over. Conflicts, so unwanted and sometimes so inopportune, may be catalysts that foster growth. They push us out of our comfort zones, making us face our weaknesses and blind spots. Each conflict can be a valuable teacher in telling us something about ourselves and our relationships, whether in a disagreement with a friend or a tense exchange at work. It is like the pearl of an oyster-sometimes it takes a little grit to find something beautiful. By embracing conflict as a learning opportunity, you transform it from a threat into a powerful personal and relational development tool.

Reflective learning is at the heart of extracting lessons from conflicts. After a disagreement, sit with your thoughts like an artist stepping back to assess their work. Post-conflict reflection exercises will help to understand what triggered the conflict and how you responded. Ask yourself, for example, what was at the root of the disagreement or how you might have contributed to it. It is not to be done for blame but to bring insight into your patterns and behaviors. You can then develop plans to deal with such situations more quickly and confidently when you recognize your triggers and responses. It's like having a personal user manual to steer the complexities of human interaction.

The advantages of honing conflict resolution skills go far beyond the immediate situation. Developing these skills enhances your resilience and adaptability, like a rubber band stretched without breaking. Whenever you resolve a conflict effectively, you build emotional muscles that serve you well in all areas of life. You learn to handle stress and keep cool in the most intense moments. Further, it's easy to bounce back after a fall with a positive attitude toward life and whatever it may bring. While working your way through conflicts with more ease, you will also find that the way you approach challenges has changed. You won't see them as impossible to surmount but as chances for growth and learning.

Putting on the glasses of a growth mindset about conflict makes everything sharper. You are not looking at a threat but an opportunity to get better. With that mindset, you are curious about the disagreement instead of being on your heels. You open yourself to feedback, learn from other people's perspectives, and refine your communication skills. This openness builds a sense of empowerment in you, knowing that conflicts do not define you; they refine you. Embracing this growth mindset, you turn conflicts into stepping stones in your path of personal development.

Moving ahead, remember that conflict is not something to be feared. It is a part of life, much like the seasons that come and go. Every conflict brings an opportunity to learn, grow, and strengthen relationships. By looking at conflicts as opportunities for growth, you create an opening to grow personally and through your relationships. What you learn from conflicts today will make for a stronger, more resilient you tomorrow. With this mindset, you will confidently march into any conflict, knowing you are prepared to transform challenges into opportunities for growth and connection.

CHAPTER SEVEN

Creating Customized Action Plans

I magine navigating a city without a map. You might find yourself lost in a maze of streets, unsure which way to turn. That's what life can feel like without clear boundaries. But fear not, for this chapter is your roadmap. Setting boundaries isn't about building walls; it's about creating bridges that lead to self-discovery and empowerment. Before you can chart your course, though, you need to know your starting point. Assessing your current boundary landscape is the first step in crafting a personalized action plan. It's like taking inventory of a garden before deciding what to plant. You need to understand where the sun shines brightest and where weeds might be creeping in.

An honest self-assessment of your boundaries reveals areas of strength and those needing a little TLC. Think of it as a spotlight illuminating the nooks and crannies of your relationships—personal and professional. Consider how effective your boundaries are with different people. Are they robust with friends but porous with family? Do they hold firm at work but falter in social settings? Identifying recurring issues can help you pinpoint where to focus your efforts. For instance, if you constantly say yes to last-minute requests, it might be time to reinforce your ability to say no. Recognizing these patterns is crucial. It's like finding the loose thread in a sweater before it unravels completely.

Comprehensive boundary assessment tools like surveys and checklists can be invaluable. A boundary assessment questionnaire, for example, might ask you to reflect on recent interactions: "Did I feel respected?" or "Was my personal time-honored?" A personal boundary inventory checklist could help you rate your comfort level in various scenarios, like attending social gatherings or responding to work emails after hours. These tools act as mirrors, reflecting your boundary landscape with clarity and precision. They provide a structured approach to self-evaluation, helping you see your boundaries from multiple angles.

Honesty is your ally in this self-assessment journey. It's tempting to gloss over the areas where boundaries falter, but actual growth comes from facing them head-on. Approach this process with openness, as if you're having a candid conversation with your best friend. Admit where boundaries crumble under pressure, and acknowledge where they've held firm. Identifying personal boundary violations is key. These are the moments when you feel your space has been encroached upon. By honestly recognizing these instances, you lay the groundwork for meaningful change.

Understanding your current boundaries sets the stage for future planning. It's like a baseline note in a symphony, grounding your efforts as you compose your boundary masterpiece. Awareness of your boundary landscape informs the steps you'll take moving forward. It highlights where you're flourishing and need to cultivate new growth. With this knowledge, you can craft an action plan that builds on your strengths and addresses areas of improvement. It's about setting realistic goals and creating a strategy that aligns with your values and aspirations.

7.2 Interactive Element: Boundary Self-Assessment Tool

Create your own Boundary Self-Assessment Tool. Start by listing key areas of your life, such as family, friends, work, and personal time. For each category, rate your satisfaction with your current boundaries on a scale from 1 to 5. Reflect on why you scored each area the way you did. Note any patterns or surprises that emerge. This tool offers a snapshot of your boundary landscape, providing insights into where to focus your customization efforts. Remember, this is a starting point, not a destination. Use it to guide your next steps as you cultivate a boundary-rich life.

7.3 Identifying Priorities and Goals

In the world of boundary setting, priorities are your guiding stars. They help you navigate through the vast universe of relationships and responsibilities. Imagine you're on a treasure hunt, and your priorities are the map that leads you to the hidden gems of self-care and well-being. But how do you determine where to focus your boundary efforts? Start by considering the emotional impact of different areas in your life. Does your heart race when you think about work demands? Do social commitments leave you feeling drained? These emotional cues are like neon signs pointing to the areas that need immediate attention. Prioritizing based on emotional impact ensures that you address the most pressing needs first, bringing relief where needed most.

Aligning your boundary priorities with personal values adds more depth to this process. Your values are the compass that guides your decisions and interactions. When your boundaries reflect your values, they become more than just limits—they become expressions of who you are. Consider what matters most to you. Is it family, honesty, or creativity? You create a cohesive, authentic framework for your life by aligning your boundaries with these core values. This alignment makes boundary setting more meaningful and strengthens your resolve to uphold them. It's like having the wind at your back, propelling you forward with purpose and clarity.

Once you've identified your priorities, it's time to set some goals. But not just any goals—SMART goals. These are Specific, Measurable, Attainable, Relevant, and Time-based. Imagine you're plotting a course on a GPS. You need to know your destination, how far it is, and the best route. SMART goals do just that for your boundaries. They provide a clear, actionable plan for establishing and maintaining limits. For instance, a SMART goal might be to "Decline one social invitation per week to prioritize self-care." This goal is specific, measurable, and time-bound, making it easier to track and achieve.

Boundary goals can be both short-term and long-term. Short-term goals are like pit stops along your journey, providing quick wins and building momentum. They include saying no to weekend work or setting aside an hour for yourself each day. Long-term goals, on the other hand, are the overarching destinations. They might involve restructuring your work-life balance or developing stronger communication skills. Both are important and create a balanced, sustainable approach to boundary setting. It's like building a house, where each short-term goal is a brick, and the long-term goals are the blueprint guiding the construction.

Flexibility is the secret ingredient in goal setting. Life is unpredictable, and priorities can change at the drop of a hat. A new job opportunity may arise, or a family situation demands your attention. Allowing for goal adjustments ensures that your boundaries remain relevant and supportive. Think of your goals as rubber bands—they need to stretch and adapt without snapping. This adaptability keeps you aligned with your current needs and circumstances, preventing the frustration and rigidity of sticking to outdated goals. It's about being responsive to the ebb and flow of life rather than rigidly adhering to a plan that no longer serves you.

Regular goal reassessment is like tuning a musical instrument. Over time, even the best-laid plans can fall out of sync with your needs. By periodically revisiting your goals, you ensure they support your growth and well-being. Consider making time each month for a boundary goal review session. Reflect on your progress, celebrate your achievements, and adjust your goals as needed. This practice keeps your boundaries/ efforts fresh and aligned with your evolving life. It's a chance to step back, evaluate, and recalibrate, ensuring that your boundaries remain strong and effective in every aspect of your life.

7.4 Crafting Your Boundary Script

Imagine a conversation where you must assert your needs clearly and confidently. Then, your personalized boundary script becomes your trusty sidekick. Crafting these scripts is like writing a play where you're both the playwright and the star. They help you articulate your boundaries consistently and with strength, ensuring you don't get lost in the heat of the moment. Having a well-thought-out script is like having a GPS for your conversation, guiding you through potential detours with ease. It ensures that your message is consistent, allowing you to express your needs without sounding like a broken record. This consistency is key, reinforcing your boundaries over time and helping others understand and respect them.

Let's break down the process of creating these scripts. First, identify key scenarios where boundaries often feel blurry. It could be declining an invitation to a social event when you'd rather recharge at home. Or setting limits with a colleague who overshares personal details during work hours. Once you've pinpointed these scenarios, draft the initial versions of your script. Start by writing down what you want to say, keeping it clear and concise. Remember, this isn't Shakespeare—it's all about directness and clarity. The beauty of drafting is that you can refine and tweak until it feels right. Think of it as editing a photo until the colors pop perfectly.

With your script in hand, it's time to practice. Role-playing with a trusted friend can be both enlightening and entertaining. It's like rehearsing lines for a play, helping you find the right tone and delivery. Practicing allows you to hear the words out loud, making adjustments where necessary. It also builds your confidence, so you're ready to deliver your lines with poise when the real conversation happens. Your friend can provide feedback, offering insights you might not have considered. This feedback is valuable, as it helps you refine your script until it feels natural and authentic.

Customization is the final touch that makes your script truly yours. Tailor your words to suit different contexts and relationships. How you set boundaries with a friend might differ from how you communicate them with a supervisor. Language and tone should reflect the nature of the relationship, ensuring your message is appropriate and respectful. For instance, a casual tone might be fitting with a close friend: "Hey, I need a bit of downtime this weekend." A more formal approach could be used professionally: "I appreciate the invitation, but I have prior commitments." This adaptability ensures your boundaries are respected across various scenarios, reinforcing your position while maintaining harmony.

Crafting boundary scripts may feel like writing dialogue for a sitcom, but the impact is anything but trivial. They provide a solid foundation for expressing your needs, helping you navigate conversations with confidence and clarity. As you practice and refine these scripts, you'll find that setting boundaries becomes second nature, an integral part of how you communicate and interact with the world.

7.5 Implementing and Testing Your Plan

Picture this: you're on a diving board, about to jump into the refreshing waters of boundary-setting. Implementing your boundary plan is much like taking that leap. It requires courage and a little bit of flair. Start with low-stakes situations to build your confidence. Think of these as your practice rounds—a friendly game before the championship. Maybe it's declining a casual coffee invite or setting a limit on evening emails. These small victories lay the groundwork for more significant boundary-setting endeavors. They're the stepping stones across the pond, each one bringing you closer to the other side of respecting your needs.

As you venture into this new territory, view these initial attempts as opportunities for growth rather than tests of your resolve. Testing boundaries is like trying on new shoes. You need to walk a few miles in them before they feel just right. Observe how others react when you assert your boundaries. Are they surprised, supportive, or somewhere in between? These reactions are like feedback from a live audience, highlighting what works and what might need tweaking. Take note of any areas where your boundaries felt too loose or tight. It's a learning process, and each experience adds a new layer to your understanding.

Gather insights from trusted individuals to evaluate how well your boundary plans are working. Think of them as personal coaches, offering an outside perspective on your performance. Ask for feedback from those who respect your journey, people who can provide constructive criticism without judgment. Perhaps a friend notices you're more relaxed after setting new limits, or a colleague appreciates your newfound assertiveness. This external validation reinforces your efforts and helps refine your approach. It's like having a mirror that reflects your progress, showing you areas of strength and those needing a bit more polish.

Through all of this, maintaining a positive mindset is your secret weapon. Resilience and positivity are like the warm-up exercises before a challenging workout, preparing you mentally and emotionally for the task. Celebrate each small success along the way. Did you manage to set a boundary without feeling guilty? High five! Did a friend respect your need for space? Do a little victory dance. These small celebrations motivate you, reminding you how far you've come and energizing you for the road ahead. They're like the confetti at a parade, adding color and joy.

Remember, the path to effective boundary-setting is not a straight line. It's a winding road with unexpected turns and delightful surprises. Embrace the journey with open arms and an open heart, knowing every step forward is a pathway to a more fulfilling life.

7.6 Adapting Boundaries to Change and Growth

Life is like a river, constantly moving and changing its course. When you think you've figured it out, a new bend appears. That's why adapting your boundaries is not just important—it's necessary. As you navigate through different stages and situations, what served you well in one phase may need adjustment in another. Imagine transitioning from high school to college, where newfound independence requires reassessing boundaries with family and friends. Or consider the shift from a single life to a committed relationship, where balancing personal time with partnership becomes crucial. These life transitions are the catalysts that prompt boundary evolution. Their gentle nudges remind you that flexibility is key to maintaining balance and well-being.

Incorporating feedback from others can be a game-changer when adjusting boundaries. Think of it like upgrading your software based on user feedback. Listening to trusted friends or family members gives insights into how your boundaries impact those around you. A friend may point out that you've become more withdrawn since starting a new job, hinting that work-life boundaries need revisiting. Or a family member notes that your assertiveness has inspired them to set boundaries. This feedback acts as a mirror, reflecting areas where you've grown and those that might benefit from more attention. It's like having a personal advisory board guiding your boundary adjustments with wisdom and care.

Annually reassessing your boundary needs can be as routine as your yearly physical check-up. It's a chance to pause and evaluate what's working and what's not. Consider this an opportunity to take stock of your current landscape, much like a gardener assessing their plot at the end of each season. Are there boundaries that have become too rigid, like overgrown hedges blocking sunlight? Or some have become too lax, allowing unwanted intrusions. This yearly evaluation helps you prune and nurture your boundaries, ensuring they continue to support your growth and well-being. It's an exercise in self-awareness, a chance to align your boundaries with the person you're becoming.

Embracing change as a growth opportunity is like welcoming an unexpected guest who is delightful company. Change can be daunting, but it also brings the potential for personal development. When you view change as a positive force, you open yourself to its possibilities. Adapting boundaries in response to change is not a sign of weakness but strength. It shows you're attuned to your needs and willing to evolve. This mindset transforms change from a source of anxiety into a catalyst for growth. It's like finding a new path in the woods that offers fresh perspectives and opportunities. With each adaptation, you strengthen your ability to respond to life's challenges with resilience and grace.

Self-reflection is the compass that guides boundary adaptation. Regular reflection illuminates the path forward, helping you clearly navigate shifting landscapes. Journaling about boundary adaptations can be a powerful tool in this process. Imagine sitting down with pen and paper, exploring how recent changes have impacted your boundaries. What new needs have emerged? How have your relationships evolved? This journaling practice acts as a dialogue with yourself, revealing insights that might otherwise remain hidden. It encourages you to be honest about your experiences, acknowledging both successes and areas for improvement. Through reflection, you gain a deeper understanding of your boundary landscape, empowering you to make informed adjustments.

Reflecting on these experiences can be like conversing with an old friend who knows you well and offers gentle guidance. It's a chance to celebrate your growth, acknowledge your challenges, and set intentions for the future. As you adapt your boundaries to fit your evolving life, remember that this process is dynamic. Just as the seasons change, so too do your needs and circumstances. Embrace this fluidity, knowing that each adjustment brings you closer to a life that's balanced, fulfilling, and uniquely yours.

Chapter Eight

Living a Balanced Life by Setting Boundaries

Think of your life as a seesaw. On one side, you have professional commitments; on the other, you have personal aspirations and relationships. Balancing can be a beautiful dance; when the end tips too far, it becomes a wild ride-one you're not signed up for. It's like trying to balance a magic trick, where one has to set boundaries so neither end comes crashing down. Business experts say that work-life balance is not just a buzzword, per se. Still, it's essential to your physical and emotional well-being and career success. Give priority to your career and life to keep life in a balance wherein the stress is minimal, and burnout may not raise its ugly head.

Setting precise work hours is putting guardrails on this seesaw, ensuring you don't tumble into a pit of exhaustion. Imagine a world where you were not forced to check emails during dinner or answer work calls on Sunday mornings. You safeguard your personal time

SETTING BOUNDARIES

from being eaten into by professional demands by defining when work starts and ends. Consider this a kind of time-blocking, just as one makes a playlist, where work and personal activities would have their single track to play independently. In this manner, neither would be overpowered by the other regarding spending time.

In any case, integrating personal and professional life isn't about multitasking at all but the creation of a symphony: the sound of every one of its constituent parts interacting. A rhythm can be initiated using routines, such as family breakfast, productive work hours, and wind-down, which might include a hobby or exercise. It would be like weaving a tapestry where work and personal interests blend seamlessly into a work of art, with every thread adding to the pattern. With these boundaries, you can say no to calls for work during your time and enjoy the moment, whether it is game night with the family or a walk in the park alone.

A clearly defined workspace is another strategy to keep work from invading your personal life. Picture having an office nook that serves as a fortress of productivity, separate from your living space. This separation helps your brain switch gears when you step away, signaling that work time is over and personal time has begun. It's like having a secret passage that whisks you from one world to another, allowing you to be fully present in whichever space you occupy. This boundary keeps work from spilling over into your home life, preserving your sanctuary.

A supportive environment at work is crucial for maintaining these boundaries. Open discussions with supervisors and colleagues about your boundary needs can foster an atmosphere of understanding. It's like being in a band where everyone knows their role, playing their part without stepping on each other's toes. By communicating your boundaries clearly, you set expectations that help balance, ensuring work is a part of your life, not all of it. Such an understanding atmosphere at work respects personal boundaries and thus allows one to grow professionally and personably.

8.2 Interactive Element: Boundary Reflection Exercise

Take a moment to reflect on your current work-life balance. Take a notebook and create a page with two columns: "Work" and "Personal." Create a list under each column. Now, decide which tasks bring joy and which are burdens. Are there particular areas where the work has created an intrusion into your personal time? Use the reflection to check on boundaries you may want to restore. Consider establishing your work hours or designation of a dedicated workspace if you have not done so already. This will help you see where adjustments should be made to keep things in balance. From there, make conscious choices about your boundaries to protect your well-being and support the growth of your career and personal interests.

8.3 Energy Management and Avoiding Burnout

Burnout is that guest that shows up uninvited and lingers too long. Knowing the early signs can help keep your life balanced. Emotional exhaustion is often the first clue, making one feel like a deflated balloon after a party: drained, spent, and with little energy to face the day. You may notice a dip in productivity, where tasks that once made you jump out of bed now feel like climbing Everest in flip-flops. Motivation, too, goes for a nosedive, and you may find yourself staring at the ceiling, trying to figure out where the enthusiasm you once had has gone. These signs are not just phases; they are that wake-up call urging you to take action before burnout becomes the reality show nobody wants to watch.

Of course, burnout is avoided by managing one's energy. Think of your energy as a bank account; you wouldn't want to overdraft it, right? In any case, rest and recharge periods will help you keep your balance healthy. Schedule breaks in your day, even if it's just a short walk or a few minutes of quiet reflection. Like hitting pause on a playlist, allowing your mind to catch its breath. Mindful breaks, breathing, and meditation miracles can work. These glimpses of serenity are like miniature pit stops along the rally of life and refuel your mental-emotional tank in no time.

The setting of boundaries is also crucial to preserve energy. It is as essential as putting guardrails around a mountain road so one would not veer off. But one way not to overcommit is to limit commitments to that fifth Zoom meeting of the day or skip a weekend outing when the couch and a good book are calling your name. This protects your time and energy and keeps you from overextending yourself and losing your balance. It's not selfish; saying no to non-essential tasks is smart. It enables you to show your attention to what is truly important, guaranteeing that you'll be able to make it with much energy, not going like a zombie in a continuous apocalypse.

Self-care is not a luxury but a necessity. It is excellent to carve out some time for self-care each day, like giving yourself a high-five daily. Take time out to engage in hobbies such as painting, gardening, or playing with your ukulele like a full-time rock star. Relaxation techniques, including yoga or a warm bath, melt away the day's stresses. These activities are the antidotes to burnout, offering moments of joy and tranquility to recharge your spirit. And remember, taking care of oneself is not selfish; it's about staying healthy and giving the best of oneself wherever needed.

Burnout does not have to be an inevitable guest. You can keep it at bay with its early recognition and proactive management. You shield yourself from modern life's relentless demands by setting boundaries, managing energy, and prioritizing self-care. That would mean building a fortress of well-being where burnout is not allowed past the drawbridge. Take a deep breath, set the boundaries, and take back your energy. Your future self will be grateful for this.

8.4 Setting Boundaries Harmonizing with Personal Values

Think about personal values as the tree roots sunk deep into your character's soil. They are stabilizing and feeding you, and just as the tree is grown from them, so should your boundaries. Boundaries align with your core beliefs and vibrant authenticity; life feels more congruent and whole. It's like making a compass that always points you toward fulfillment, and decisions don't feel so much like a maze but rather a well-marked trail.

You must first understand what matters most to you to align your boundaries with your values. This is somewhat of a process of introspection, like a personal treasure hunt for what's at the core of your belief system. One of these valuable exercises is a values clarification worksheet. The point of a values clarification worksheet is to guide and aid in determining what values define you. Values clarification worksheets may ask questions like, "What activities do you most often lose track of time for?" or "For what do you stand, even when it requires

SETTING BOUNDARIES

standing alone?" Such reflection encourages discovering your most essential values, on which your boundary-setting work shall stand.

Once you have defined your values, establishing boundaries and supporting them would be a natural progression. It seems like a pretty good next step: reflective journaling about decisions that align with those values follows suit. Think of it as letters to your future self: how you want to live and which boundaries support those wishes. In these journal entries, you might find that family time is essential. Thus, you put boundaries on your work hours, or that creativity feeds your soul; therefore, you create boundaries to protect your creative time. In this way, reflection turns abstract values into concrete guidelines by which to live your life.

Making value-aligned boundaries means designing decision-making frameworks based on your values. Imagine being in a paradigm where every decision is weighed against a set of core values that you have, rather like a chef who tastes something and knows right away whether it is correct. When any boundary decision does not feel right, revisit the choice and consider what makes you feel good. Such practice heightens your sense of authenticity and integrity, whereby you will live to the best of your beliefs. It's like wearing a perfectly tailored suit: You feel comfortable and confident; everything fits.

However, value-aligned boundaries do much more than merely make people happy with themselves. They guarantee a life of purpose and direction in that your actions speak the truth about who you are inside. The result is an experience of wholeness and satisfaction, going through life with a sense of coherence in identity. It's like tuning an instrument to the right pitch, where everything harmonizes in beauty. With these boundaries in place, you experience an increased sense of authenticity, knowing your life resonates with the melody of your values.

8.5 Textual Element: Values and Boundaries Checklist

Create a checklist to help solidify your value-aligned boundaries. Start by listing your top five core values. Next, identify existing boundaries that reflect these values and note any areas lacking alignment. This checklist serves as a reminder of your commitment to living authentically. Revisit it regularly, especially when faced with decisions that challenge your boundaries. Let it guide you, ensuring your boundaries remain true to your core beliefs. This practice strengthens your values and gives you the strength to build a life reflecting on yourself.

These can also help you to make your boundaries not merely acts of reactions but proactive affirmations of principles one may hold. In this process, as you align your boundaries to your values, you have actually started building a life that is not only rewarding but meaningful, too. Step into alignment, and let your life transform into an alive tapestry interwoven with your values and boundaries.

8.6 Flexibility and Adaptability

Visualize living in a world where your boundaries are as rigid as a granite wall. They may protect you yet simultaneously confine you. Life is not a statue; it is a flux, like the flowing of a river, so your boundaries, too, need to learn how to float on it. Flexible boundaries will be like a well-tailored suit, adjusting to life's demands while retaining their core structure. They enable you to respond to life transitions, whether a new job, changed family dynamics, or personal growth. These adjustments help your boundaries stay relevant and supportive, considering how your circumstances might change.

Developing flexibility within boundaries involves an open-minded attitude. It is similar to tuning an instrument; sometimes, you must make minor adjustments to keep everything in harmony. Begin with the practice of open-mindedness. Whenever change comes knocking, ask yourself, "How can I shift my boundaries so they serve me better now?" This question invites an openness to explore new possibilities. For instance, if your job requires you to put in extra hours temporarily, you may need to relax the boundaries around time but pull in those related to self-care to maintain your equilibrium. Flexibility doesn't mean compromising your needs; it involves creativity in how you meet them.

A balance between rigidity and flexibility must be struck. But when this goes too far, the walls may become the barriers to further growth. If they're too flexible, they won't offer much protection. The effectiveness of your boundaries needs occasional reevaluation: do they get you through or hold you back in life? Check-in with yourself as though it were a boundary checkup to ensure they are healthy and serving you. When you observe which of your boundaries no longer serves you, ask yourself, should I give them a tune-up? This balance will keep your boundaries effective, changing with your needs.

Change is often considered a disruptor, but change can be a facilitator, too. When you begin to embrace change as a positive force, you will then be able to see boundary evolution not as a loss but as an opportunity. You celebrate your adaptability as a strength: every time you change your boundaries to fit better into your life, you show resilience. It's like upgrading your phone's software; it gets more functional and modern every time. So, consider these changes personal achievements and acknowledge them as growth milestones.

8.7 Visual Element: Flexibility Spectrum Chart

Create a Flexibility Spectrum Chart to visualize your boundaries and their flexibility. First, draw a line with "Rigid" and "Flexible" on either end. Place your boundaries on that line. You will then better understand which boundary needs more give and which has more structure. Revisit this chart regularly, especially during life transitions, to ensure your boundaries continue serving you.

As you learn to live with flexible boundaries, remember that it is not a weakness but a testimony to how well you can handle the dynamics of life. They allow you to graciously rise with the changes so your boundaries continue to serve you. You create a resilient, flourishing life in which change is your ally, not your enemy, through continued change according to your needs. Your boundaries develop into a living structure where you are guided through the ups and downs with confidence and clarity.

8.8 Long-Term Health Maintenance

Boundaries are the unsung heroes of long-term health that happen silently behind the scenes to keep you healthy and content. Setting boundaries works like a well-oiled machine, constantly allowing your life to run smoothly. Without these invisible lines, life can quickly become an all-you-can-eat buffet where you're trying to balance too many plates and risk a spectacular and messy spill. Establishing routines that support mental and physical health is one way to keep those plates in check. Maybe it's walking briskly each morning, taking a minute to meditate, or perhaps ending with a good book instead of scrolling through social media. These routines are the anchors that keep you grounded in the storm of everyday requests and provide you with a consistent framework that supports your well-being.

Wellness should be incorporated into your daily routine to care for your well-being. Think of it as a recipe where the main ingredients, in this case, are balanced. It's about finding the right balance between work and rest, like a good playlist with fast and slow beats. Let your day be about balancing work and pleasure together, melding a dose of yoga into your tasks, or enjoying your hobby after dinner. The essence is that this balanced approach will prevent you from going into burnout and keep you refreshed like a battery being refueled rather than used up. Besides helping deter stress, incorporating wellness practices adds an upward beat to the quality of your life; with that, you know you're revitalized and prepared for whatever crosses your path.

Regular self-assessment helps maintain wellness. Visualize this as a monthly checkup, like taking your car in for a mechanic check. It's your time to ensure everything is in good working order and take care of any potential issues before they become huge. Monthly wellness checks can be as simple as carving out time for reflection regarding how your boundaries are working for you. Are they still serving you well, or is it time to make some adjustments? This way, you can stop boundary breaches before they escalate into significant issues, like patching up that small leak before it floods the basement. You will ensure that your boundaries align with your life as it changes, providing a good core for continued well-being.

Beyond personal practices, nurturing a supportive community is essential. Surround yourself with people who respect and support your boundaries-think a cheering section to aid in one's success. The network supports and reinforces those tested boundaries, so if it were within your means, then join these groups or communities of people where boundaries are praised and shared. Be it a book club, hobby group, or online forum, being part of a community helps put value into personal boundaries. These networks remind one that they are not alone in balancing everything out, giving them a sense of belonging and encouragement. You build a support network. You create an environment that allows your well-being to thrive, supported by the combined strength of those who understand and respect your boundaries.

Imagine living a life where boundaries were not only considered but celebrated. A life where your needs weren't just heard but accommodated by every person in your community. This is not some pipe dream but is created by setting a consistent boundary and fostering a life of well-being. Your joy and health are not optional privileges but requirements nurtured by the limits you set in life and community.

8.9 Inspiring Others Through Your Boundary Journey

When you model healthy boundaries, it's like planting seeds in a garden. Those around you observe how you navigate life, and your actions can inspire them to cultivate their own boundaries. Leading by example is one of the most potent ways to make a statement personally and professionally. Imagine being in a meeting where everybody is scrambling for more work, and you confidently state your limits. Your coworkers may raise an eyebrow initially, but they see the positive effects over time. It's not just the no's—it's teaching others it's okay to say no without feeling guilty. This inspires change in people around you; this could trigger something for them to set boundaries and work on healthier habits.

You can inspire others by sharing your success stories regarding setting boundaries. Think of it like sitting around the campfire, telling stories to entertain and teach. Community forums and blogs are great for this. Sharing your experiences, successes, and struggles may provide valuable insights for those just starting out on their boundary-setting journeys. When you share how you finally gained the confidence to say no to that additional project, others can relate to having struggled similarly. Your story will serve as a beacon to help them navigate the uncertainty and clarify that they do not have to walk alone. They can also be flexible with their situations. Sharing your journey will inspire others and reinforce your commitment to building and maintaining healthy boundaries.

Mentoring and supporting those new at setting boundaries is likened to being an experienced traveler who gives novices valuable tips. You get to lead peers or mentees through their boundary-setting journeys, which could be anything from a friend not knowing how to stand up for themselves against an overbearing boss to a younger sibling at school not knowing how to say no to peer pressure. You get to mentor them from experience and encourage them when things do not go well. This role is never about telling them what to do but walking alongside them and lending a hand when necessary. In mentoring others, you reinforce your understanding of boundaries and build a community where respect and balance are paramount.

The impact of your boundary work can have ripples far beyond your immediate circle. Just as one pebble thrown into a body of water creates ever-expanding ripples, so will your commitment to boundaries, translating into more significant cultural shifts toward respect and balance. One potential ripple effect may be engaging in boundary education advocacy. This might mean speaking at local events, writing articles, or even advocating at work for the importance of boundaries. These actions add to a more significant movement in which boundaries become an accepted and appreciated part of life. Your work creates a world where people are empowered to claim their needs without fear, and mutual respect is the order of the day.

As you continue setting and maintaining your boundaries, keep in mind the depth of your reach into the people around you. Whether by setting examples, sharing stories, mentoring others, or spearheading societal change, you leave the world in a better-balanced, respectful place. Your journey is not purely personal but a stimulant to transformation for others. Enter this identity, and watch the seeds that you plant in the garden of positive changes flower into where limits are celebrated and people can thrive.

As we close this chapter, remember that you are on a trip to set boundaries- a tapestry interfaced with personal growth, resilience, and empowerment at every turn. Each boundary set is one stitch in this tapestry; the pattern reflects your values and priorities. Keep learning about and redefining your limits as you go along, bearing in mind that by doing so, you inspire others to help create a world where respect and balance are cherished. Now, let's see how these principles apply in the specific areas of life and thus enable one to move with confidence and clarity in relationships.

Conclusion

As we near the close of our time together, take a moment to consider how setting boundaries can impact and even powerfully change your life. Consider that boundaries are guardrails along a twisting road, guiding you to destinations of self-empowerment and healthier relationships. They are not limitations but keys to a balanced and whole life.

Throughout this book, we have learned the intricate dance of setting boundaries. We have analyzed boundary types: physical, emotional, mental, and many more, each serving as a different tool in your empowerment toolkit. We have looked at how one must overcome internal obstacles like the fear of conflict or guilt that comes with self-care. Remember, setting boundaries isn't selfish; it's about honoring your worth and protecting your well-being.

Of course, communication has played a starring role in all of this. From assertive language to non-verbal display, we have equipped you with the tools to state your needs clearly and confidently so that your limits are heard and respected. And, of course, there is mindfulness and self-reflection. These are like tuning forks, helping you stay attuned to your needs and adapt your boundaries as life unfolds. Every time you breathe with awareness or take the time to write in your journal, you bring clarity and affirmation to your commitment to be yourself.

Conflict resolution strategies empower you to approach life's inevitable disagreements with poise and wisdom. Whether by negotiating or de-escalating, these tools keep harmony in your relationships while preserving personal integrity. Remember that conflicts are not roadblocks but opportunities for growth and understanding.

Custom action plans are your success roadmap. In tailoring boundary-setting strategies to your unique circumstances, you lay the groundwork for sustained progress. Monitoring your growth ensures that your boundaries will be effective and continue to meet your changing needs. It's like tending a garden: regular care and attention yield a bountiful harvest.

Boundaries are your compass in the quest for holistic balance. They help you merge personal and professional commitments without feeling overwhelmed by either. This keeps the balance in life to avoid burnout and live a life where joy and productivity coexist.

Setting boundaries is not an act but a lifelong process of growth, adaptation, and strengthening. Embrace this journey, knowing that every step will fortify your ability to lead a fulfilling life. Start small, perhaps by saying no to one request that doesn't align with your priorities. Gradually expand your boundary-setting repertoire, celebrating each victory along the way.

There are many stories of successful boundary-setting, each giving inspiration and motivation. Take, for example, the story of Alex, who changed their work-life balance by setting clear boundaries with their employer, or Jamie, who learned to express their needs effectively and found more authentic and rewarding relationships. These stories tell you that change is possible and that your efforts can bring about similarly positive results.

As you begin, remember that you are not in this alone. Reach out within your community for support, sharing experiences and insights that will promote a culture of healthy boundary-setting. We can make together a world where boundaries are appreciated and respected, adding to the well-being of all individuals.

Before I close, I want to express my deepest gratitude for your commitment to this journey. Your efforts at setting and maintaining boundaries will affect your life and the lives of people around you. Thank you for allowing me to be part of your journey toward empowerment. Remember, you have within you the strength and wisdom to conduct your life with confidence, clarity, and compassion. The road ahead is yours, and I am confident you will thrive.

References

- *Overcoming Boundary Issues: A Guide To Healthy Dynamics* https://mindowl.org/boundary-issues/

- *The Importance of Personal Boundaries - Psych Central* https://psychcentral.com/relationships/the-importance-of-personal-boundaries

- *7 Myths About Setting Boundaries* https://makedapennycooke.com/7-myths-setting-boundaries/

- *7 Signs Someone Doesn't Respect Your Boundaries and ...* https://psychcentral.com/relationships/signs-boundary-violations

- *The Fictitious Reality of Avoiding Conflict | Psychology Today* https://www.psychologytoday.com/us/blog/explorations-in-positive-psychology/202310/the-fictitious-reality-of-avoiding-conflict

- *Group-based shame, guilt, and regret across cultures - PMC* https://pmc.ncbi.nlm.nih.gov/articles/PMC9306671/ Learn how to stop being a people pleaser with these 10 tips https://www.calm.com/blog/how-to-stop-being-a-people-pleaser

- *Setting boundaries for well-being - Mayo Clinic Health System* https://www.mayoclinichealthsystem.org/hometown-health/speaking-of-health/setting-boundaries-for-well-being

- *Communication and Boundaries - Center for Mindful Therapy* https://mindfulcenter.org/communication-and-boundaries/

- *How to Say No Assertively to a Request for Your Time* https://www.psychologytoday.com/us/blog/speak-easy/201709/how-to-say-no-assertively-to-a-request-for-your-time

- *Setting Non-Verbal Boundaries In Your Life - NICOLE OHME* - https://nicoleohme.ch/site/setting-non-verbal-boundaries-in-your-life

- *How to Handle the Reactions of Others to Your New ...* https://lorengelberggoff.com/dealing-with-the-consequences-how-to-handle-the-reactions-of-others-to-your-new-boundaries/

- *The sensitivity of boundary setting in collectivist cultures* https://www.counseling.org/publications/counseling-today-magazine/article-archive/article/legacy/the-sensitivity-of-boundary-setting-in-collectivist-cultures

- *3 Kind, Simple & Effective Ways to Communicate Your ...* https://organizations.headspace.com/blog/3-kind-simple-effective-ways-to-communicate-your-boundaries

- *Building Social Media Boundaries | Blog* https://www.talktoangel.com/blog/building-social-media-boundaries

- *Setting Boundaries at Work: A Key to Well-Being* https://www.lyrahealth.com/blog/setting-boundaries-at-work/

- *How to Set Mindful Boundaries - Mastermind Meditate* https://www.mastermindmeditate.com/blog/how-to-set-mindful-boundaries

- *Mental Health Benefits of Journaling* https://www.webmd.com/mental-health/mental-health-benefits-of-journaling

- *Mindfulness meditation: A research-proven way to reduce ...* https://www.apa.org/topics/mindfulness/meditation

- *The Importance of Mindful Communication for Mental Health* https://www.verywellmind.com/mindful-communication-definition-principles-benefits-how-to-do-it-7489103

- *Conflict Resolution Skills* https://www.helpguide.org/relationships/communication/conflict-resolution-skills

- *The Role of Empathy in Negotiation* https://www.redbearnegotiation.com/blog/role-of-empathy

- *De-escalation Techniques: 30 Proven Strategies to Diffuse ...* https://blog.hubspot.com/service/de-escalation-techniques

SETTING BOUNDARIES

- *How to Set Boundaries in Your Relationships* https://psychcentral.com/relationships/why-healthy-relationships-always-have-boundaries

- *14 Worksheets for Setting Healthy Boundaries* https://positivepsychology.com/healthy-boundaries-worksheets/

- *Smart Goals for Setting Boundaries - GoalSetting.online* https://goalsetting.online/articles/smart-goals-for-setting-boundaries.html

- *How to Set Healthy Boundaries: A Guide with Real-Life ...* https://innertravelcoaching.com/blog/6237/how-to-set-healthy-boundaries-a-guide-with-real-life-scripts

- *8 Tips on Setting Boundaries for Your Mental Health - DBSA* https://www.dbsalliance.org/support/young-adults/8-tips-on-setting-boundaries-for-your-mental-health.

- *How to Improve Your Work-Life Balance Today* https://www.businessnewsdaily.com/5244-improve-work-life-balance-today.html

- *7 early signs of burnout and how to avoid it - Livi* https://www.livi.co.uk/your-health/7-early-signs-of-burnout/

- *Good Boundaries Start With Strong Values* https://www.centerforsharedinsight.com/blog/boundaries-start-strong-values/13385

- *How Setting Flexible Boundaries Can Help Dispel Burnout ...* https://www.millennialtherapy.com/anxiety-therapy-blog/flexible-

www.ingramcontent.com/pod-product-compliance
Lightning Source LLC
Chambersburg PA
CBHW062125040426
42337CB00044B/4091